COCKATIELS

HOWARD RICHMOND

As parrots and parrot-like birds are becoming more and more popular, a need for information regarding their diet, behavior and breeding habits is on the rise. This book can supply all that and more on one of the parrot world's most popular members—the cockatiel.

The cockatiel is a medium-sized Australian parrot, averaging 12-14 inches from the top if its head to the tip of its tail. Because of its size, it is becoming a very popular household pet. It has come to exist in various distinctive color varieties, which give it quite a different appearance from the wild grey it originated from. And it proves to be a very affectionate companion to the whole family.

Most people enjoy the companionship of cockatiels. They have agreeable personalities and are intelligent as well as affectionate. The cockatiel makes an ideal pet for those who wish a bird larger than a budgie yet smaller than an amazon. A cockatiel can truly become one's best friend!

Photography by: Dr. Herbert R. Axelrod, Glen S Axelrod, Horst Bielfeld, R. Brega, Michael DeFeitas, Isabelle Francais, Michael Gilroy, E. Goldfinger, John Manzione, Robert Pearcy, N. Richmond, Vince Serbin, Ronald R. Smith, Louise B. Van der Meid, Wayne Wallace, and R. Williams

© T.F.H. Publications, Inc.

Distributed in the UNITED STATES to the Pet Trade by T.F.H. Publications, Inc., 1 TFH Plaza, Neptune City, NJ 07753; on the Internet at www.tfh.com; in CANADA by Rolf C. Hagen Inc., 3225 Sartelon St., Montreal, Quebec H4R 1E8; Pet Trade by H & L Pet Supplies Inc., 27 Kingston Crescent, Kitchener, Ontario N2B 2T6; in ENGLAND by T.F.H. Publications, PO Box 74, Havant PO9 5TT; in AUSTRALIA AND THE SOUTH PACIFIC by T.F.H. (Australia), Pty. Ltd., Box 149, Brookvale 2100 N.S.W., Australia; in NEW ZEALAND by Brooklands Aquarium Ltd., 5 McGiven Drive, New Plymouth, RD1 New Zealand; in SOUTH AFRICA by Rolf C. Hagen S.A. (PTY.) LTD., P.O. Box 201199, Durban North 4016, South Africa; in JAPAN by T.F.H. Publications, Japan—Jiro Tsuda, 10-12-3 Ohjidai, Sakura, Chiba 285, Japan. Published by T.F.H. Publications, Inc.

MANUFACTURED IN THE
UNITED STATES OF AMERICA
BY T.F.H. PUBLICATIONS, INC.

PARROTS QUARTERLY

yearBOOKS, INC.
Glen S. Axelrod
Chief Executive Officer

Gary Hersch
Executive Vice President

Barry Duke
Chief Operating Officer

Marilee Talman
Editor-in-Chief

Linda Lindner
Editor

DIGITAL PRE-PRESS
Patricia Northrup
Supervisor

Robert Onyrscuk
Jose Reyes
Digital Pre-Press Production

COMPUTER ART
Patti Escabi
Candida Moreira

ADVERTISING SALES
Nancy S. Rivadeneira
Advertising Sales Director
Cheryl J. Blyth
Chris O' Brien
Advertising Account Managers
Adrienne Rescinio
Advertising Production Manager
Frances Wrona
Advertising Coordinator

©yearBOOKS, Inc.
1 TFH Plaza
Neptune, N.J. 07753
Completely manufactured in Neptune, N.J.
USA

Contents

Feeding and Housing 15

Cockatiels as Pets 3

Taming and Training ... 38

Cockatiel Care 29

Breeding Cockatiels 51

Your Cockatiel's Good Health 58

Suggested Reading 64

COCKATIELS AS PETS

Cockatiels are very affectionate birds that quickly become wonderful companions for the entire family.

If you walk into any pet shop that sells birds, you are sure to find many birds that are members of the parrot order. Some of these brightly colored creatures are well-known for their ability to imitate the human voice, some for their brilliant plumage, and others for their affectionate personalities. Of the many pet birds usually available in pet shops, cockatiels seem to be ideal pets: highly personable, exhibiting amusing antics, easy to care for, and having a talent for mimicry. This graceful, distinctively colored parrot, known to science as *Nymphicus hollandicus, is* often called a "quarrion" in Australia. Second only to budgerigars in popularity, cockatiels may be purchased at a relatively low cost, are easy to tame and train, and excel as household pets. Cockatiels continue to gain wide acceptance among owners of pet birds.

Ancient history tells of many instances in which parrots were kept as pets. They had been brought from India to ancient Greece. Romans too brought parrots back to their native land from Africa. Later, European explorers, venturing into tropical countries new to them, found native Indians keeping tamed parrots as household pets. Still, although parrots had been kept as pets for many hundreds of years, it was only with the introduction of Australian species, including cockatiels and budgerigars, that parrots attracted wide attention. The popularity of cockatiels and budgerigars soon spread throughout the world.

One of the most readily distinguished groups of parrots, because of anatomy, is the cockatoos. All are native to the Pacific region. They stand out because of their movable crests and subtle coloration. They never have the bright colors many other parrots do. Many believe that the smallest of the cockatoos is the cockatiel. The crest bears this out, but there is a considerable difference in appearance between the long-tailed cockatiel and the larger, more stockily built, short-tailed cockatoos.

Although larger than a parakeet, the cockatiel is not as large as its parrot relatives. This makes it a nice sized bird for those that are just beginning in the hobby.

COCKATIELS AS PETS

In the wild, cockatiels feed on seedling grasses, buds, fruits and nuts. There is a wide variety available to them in their homeland. It is important that we, as owners, try to simulate this diet as much as possible.

THE WILD COCKATIEL

The cockatiel is indigenous to Australia. In their native habitat, they travel and nest in flocks, often in the same areas as budgerigars. The cockatiel leads a nomadic existence. Ranging through openly forested areas and savannas in the arid central regions of the continent, cockatiels feed on the seeds of a number of grasses, varied herbage such as leaves and bark, as well as fruits and berries. The availability of water to a great extent determines their wanderings; often they must cover vast areas in order to survive. Being nomadic, they may appear almost anywhere throughout the interior of Australia, but they usually avoid the coastal areas except in periods of extreme drought.

In the wild they may breed more often than once a year, the frequency being dependent upon the food supply. It is not unusual for a large flock of cockatiels to remain for some time in an area offering favorable living conditions, perhaps rearing several broods in succession. When the growing number of young birds or the changing season begins to limit the available food supply, most of the birds move on.

The rapid growth of vegetation resulting from the rainy season usually triggers the start of breeding. Cockatiels nest in hollows in the trunks of trees. Should the cavity be too small, the birds use their beaks to scoop out the soft parts of the tree. Most often they choose a nest location that affords them a good view in all directions.

Like budgerigars, they are opportunistic breeders and are inclined to breed in captivity whenever the conditions are right. As a result, cockatiels have become widely available as pets. To satisfy the demand for pet birds, many large commercial breeding operations have come into being. Because of the growth of commercial breeding, as well as the prohibition on exporting birds from Australia, no cockatiel that you encounter will be wild caught. All will have been bred in captivity.

COCKATIELS AS COMPANIONS

It is because cockatiels are well adapted to the vicissitudes of a relatively harsh environment that they are successful as cage birds. They are accustomed to a diet that is simple (compared to that demanded by many bird species) and the components of this diet are items that those who keep the birds can easily supply. In addition to being hardy by nature and easy to feed, cockatiels are clean birds requiring only minimum care.

One of the characteristics that adds a great deal to the attraction of pet cockatiels is that they enjoy being stroked about the head. They do not seem to mind being handled as much as some other bird species, and may even enjoy

Cockatiels enjoy the companionship of other birds and of humans. If you cannot be home all day, you may wish to consider purchasing two birds to keep each other company.

COCKATIELS AS PETS

being picked up. This derives from their natural behavior: normally living in small flocks in the wild, the cockatiel is essentially a social bird. They are so gregarious that when the flock settles on a dead tree, most birds perch together on the same branch. This sociable behavior evident in the wild becomes an attachment to the bird keeper in captivity.

Like other parrots, cockatiels are very capable climbers because of the structure of their feet. Also, they use their hooked bill as a third foot to pull themselves forward among branches or along tree trunks. This tendency to use the bill as a means of locomotion, combined with climbing activities and their inclination toward preening, results in a number of highly amusing antics, often endearing the bird to its owner. Here again natural behaviors are the foundation for the appeal birds like cockatiels have as pets.

Cockatiels are one of many species of parrots that can be taught to imitate human words with amazing fidelity. There is no evidence that parrots ever use their remarkable powers of imitation in the wild, but in captivity, when kept in close contact with human beings

Cockatiels are among the most inexpensive parrot-like birds on the market and are available in most pet shops. They are very adaptable birds that tame easily and are relatively quiet.

but away from their own kind, many individuals will mimic their human keepers. They soon learn that the vocalization of words they often hear results in an increase in the amount of attention they receive from their human companions. It's likely that the learning of human speech by pet birds stems from their need for social relationship.

For some people, a parrot alone in its cage is a sad sight. They feel it needs a companion. However, if a single cockatiel has adequate human companionship, it will not be lonely. This means that if you are planning to keep a single cockatiel, you must give it the attention it needs. The happiest single birds are those that do become tame and interact with their owners. Untamed birds usually are neglected. If you find that you are unable to tame your cockatiel, or that you no longer have the time to keep it company, then obtaining a second cockatiel can be the solution. Two cockatiels kept together will be much more interested in one another than they are in you. This is particularly true if they are male and female for cockatiels are inclined to form strong pair bonds.

You must have your purpose for owning a cockatiel clear in mind before you go shopping for one. If you desire a cockatiel that will be an affectionate pet, then we recommend purchasing a single bird. This book, then, is written for the person who wants to keep a single pet cockatiel. The considerations involved in keeping pairs or colonies of cockatiels—for breeding, perhaps—are not discussed here.

A cockatiel's diet should include a seed mixture, available from your local pet store, as well as plenty of fresh fruits and vegetables.

SHOPPING FOR A PET

In shopping for a pet cockatiel, you will be fortunate if you are able to choose from several sources. Outlets specializing in birds are more likely to stock outstanding individual cockatiels. While some sources may sell only livestock, others will offer one-stop shopping. Besides the cockatiel, you will need food, a cage, and various accessories. It certainly is advantageous to purchase your cockatiel from a nearby location so that the seller of the bird can be consulted for additional advice. You will want to deal with people who are able to give you satisfactory, knowledgeable answers to your questions.

It is essential that you patronize an establishment where the birds are kept under the very best of conditions. Perhaps above all else, cleanliness of the place where you plan to buy your cockatiel should be a primary consideration. As you visit the places where birds are sold, look for a clean situation, where the general appearance of the birds is one of health. Look for well-maintained cages. Food and water containers should also reflect daily care. Since clean conditions are essential to the well-being of any living creature, you will want to purchase your cockatiel from an environment that shows the birds have been carefully maintained and cared for in sanitary surroundings.

YOUNGSTERS FOR TAMING

It is generally agreed that a bird to be kept as a pet should be acquired when it is young. Have you ever wondered why? For all birds the weeks after they leave the nest are a most important period. It is during this time that they learn to adapt to the environment in which they find themselves. It is also at this time that the birds are most receptive to taming and training. They can also be taught to sample various foods.

The tamest and most affectionate cockatiels are those that have been hand-reared. These youngsters become attached to the person taking over the role of parent, and this affection for people is transferred to other owners.

Cockatiels are very sociable birds, however, they make better pets if kept singly.

It's also possible that breeders give frequent handling to cockatiel nestlings, even though they are still being fed by their natural parents; these youngsters are also especially tame. Obtaining a tame cockatiel may be worth quite a lot to you, for it can save you time. If you should be able to find such a bird, expect to pay a bit more money for it.

You can tell if a bird is somewhat tame, as it will not become too excited when a person approaches the cage. If you wish to see if a cockatiel is hand-tamed, insert your hand into the cage very slowly, palm down. Move the side of your hand towards the bird's feet. If it calmly accepts this approach, it has probably been hand-tamed.

Most of the cockatiels you encounter will probably be tame. You will therefore not have to do the taming and training yourself. Many of the birds now available are hand-fed babies and have known nothing but handling and cuddling since practically right out of the egg! Older birds, or birds that have not been hand-fed can still become good pets, but it's likely to require more effort on your part.

A cockatiel younger than six weeks of age may not be

COCKATIELS AS PETS

Cockatiels make the best pets if purchased at a young age. Birds that are 10-12 weeks are now available from pet stores.

completely self-feeding yet. While it's rare that too young a bird is offered for sale, you must be certain that the bird is able to eat on its own.

There are several indicators that can give you an adequate idea of a cockatiel's age. In general, juveniles have less dense feathering than adults, so they look slimmer. Often this more sparse feathering is most obvious in the crest. But for our purposes, the beak gives the best clues: it will change from pinkish to gray in the period between 8-12 weeks of age, approximately. The youngest suitable candidates therefore will have bills that show some gray (of course, this will not occur in those color varieties in which dark pigment is suppressed).

Around about six months of age, most cockatiels will have attained adult plumage, which is most apparent in the brightness of the cheek patches, particularly of the males. For a more exact knowledge of a cockatiel's age, you will have to rely upon the person from whom you purchase the bird. Not only is the seller in a better position to know, but he likely has also had a great deal more experience in judging age.

Many prospective pet owners are interested in how long the animal will live. There are reports of cockatiels alive at 25, but this is equivalent to people living until they are a hundred. It's more realistic to think of your cockatiel living for 10-15 years.

SEXING COCKATIELS

Determination of the sex of a juvenile cockatiel is next to impossible. This is because young males and females both have the feathering and coloration of a female until they experience their first molt. Although a number of features in a growing bird seem to be indicative of sex, none are foolproof. For this reason it is thought not to be important to discuss methods of sexing that are not always valid. Additionally, it makes little difference whether you obtain a male or a female for a family pet. They are equally lovable, and one is as fascinating as the other. Both can be tamed and trained easily, and both make equally fine pets—though some authorities feel that a male cockatiel will be superior to a female in talking ability.

After the molt, which occurs when the birds are around six months old, the differences between the sexes becomes obvious, in most varieties of cockatiels at least. Cockatiels that have the coloration found in the wild are called "Normals." The

Be certain the cockatiel you choose is old enough and is eating on his own before you bring him home. This young cockatiel is too young, however, only a few more weeks are needed before he is ready to come live with you.

A beautiful normal grey male. Regardless of color variety, the cockatiel remains basically the same interesting and intelligent pet. Each bird is as individual in its personality as we humans are.

basic color is dark gray, with a prominent white patch of feathers on the wings. The head is capped by a crest, and the bill, eyes, and feet of mature birds are black. The distinctive features of the male are the bright orange cheek patch and the yellow coloring on the head. The crest is a mixture of yellow and gray. The total length of the male is about 13 inches. Generally, the body color of the hen is much like that of the cock; however, the plumage is duller and less distinctive. She can easily be differentiated from the male by the barred pattern on the undersides of the wing and tail feathers.

COLOR VARIETIES

The coloration of the Normal cockatiel is produced by two groups of pigments, called *melanins* and *carotenoids*. The melanins produce the gray color of the Normal, while the yellow is a carotenoid. The orange of the cheek patch is probably a carotenoid too. Variation in the deposit of these pigments in the feathers is responsible for the differences in appearance in mutation cockatiels. In the "Pied" and the "Pearl," melanin is absent from certain feathers, or areas of feathers, as compared to the Normal. With the "Lutino," melanin is completely absent from the feathers, so the

Two of the first mutations to occur were the pied and the lutino varieties.

persisting carotenoids become more visible. On the other hand, it is the carotenoids that are absent from the "Whiteface," so its appearance is due entirely to the presence of melanins. If both pigments were absent, the result would be a true albino cockatiel. This variety has been achieved recently, by combining the genetic factors responsible for the Lutino and the White-face.

All these color varieties have occurred in captivity. The earliest are by now well established and are frequently available. Most common are Lutinos, Pieds, and Pearls.

Lutino

Comprising of individuals that range from almost white to a good yellow, the lutino is one of the most popular varieties. As we've said earlier, this variety is not a true albino; even to call it white is misleading. Color is still present, in the orange cheek patch for example, and there is always at least a tinge of yellow in the plumage. Because of the lack of pigment in their eyes, Lutinos often appear to be sensitive to bright light.

When this variety first appeared, it took the avicultural world by storm because it so closely resembled a miniature white cockatoo with a pale yellow crest and an almost white body, tail, and wings.

In the male bird, the least yellow is found in the areas

A lutino cinnamon pearl. This cockatiel encompasses a number of different varieties, the lutino, the cinnamon and the pearl.

COCKATIELS AS PETS

No matter what color variety cockatiel you purchase, all cockatiels are elegant looking birds with their erect carriage and magnificent crests.

that are gray in the Normal cockatiel. The throat, part of the cheeks, and the front of the head are lemon yellow. The crest is a mixture of yellow and white, and the ear-patches are the normal shade of red-orange. The wings have areas of yellow and there is a yellow cast or tinge on the tail. The eyes are red, the beak is a yellow horn color, and the legs and feet are flesh pink.

Although diffficult to sex at a distance, the adult hens, however light, still show some of the yellow barring on the undersides of the tail and the wings.

The pearl mutation was actually an unexpected happening. Breeders are learning how to perfect this mutation and are creating more and more variations of it.

Pearl

The Pearl cockatiel exhibits a change of pattern on the feathers. In this variety the nape of the neck, mantle, and the upper wing coverts are the areas always affected, the feathers exhibiting a scalloped effect. The same pattern is sometimes found on the breast. The Pearl effect results from white or pale yellow feathers that are edged in gray and also contain a small gray area in the center of each feather.

While the Pearl markings are found on all young birds, the cock birds lose them after the first molt. Most Pearl males can be distinguished from Normal males during the first year because they continue to carry a few pale, flecked feathers on the back or the shoulders. Also, most males will carry a slight amount of yellow at the base of each tail feather.

Breeding two different color varieties together does not guarantee what the offspring will be unless the two birds are pure for their variety.

Pied

Pied cockatiels show great variance in markings. Those birds having mostly clear feathers in the wings, tail, head, and chest are considered "good" Pieds. The desired symmetrical pattern, the same on both sides of the bird, is rarely seen. No two birds are exactly alike.

The Pied male is similar in color to the Normal and has clear patches of differing sizes that interrupt the dark color. These clear, irregularly shaped patches are either white or yellow tinted with white. The beak and eyes are like those of a Normal, but the feet and legs may be gray, pink, or a mixture of both.

COCKATIELS AS PETS

The albino cockatiel. Albinos lack the trace of all pigment, including in the eye.

Other Varieties

The following cockatiel varieties are becoming more popular to the avicultural world and are now quite well established. In the "Cinnamon," the melanin pigment is brown, not black, so the birds have a tarnish color. The male is a darker shade than the female. An even lighter brown shade is found in "Fallow" cockatiels. The Fallow can be conceived of as a dilute version of the Cinnamon; similarly, the "Silver" shows the gray of the Normal in a lighter, diluted form.

The most recent genetic change in cockatiels is responsible for the White-face. This variety is unique in that it does not have the orange cheek patch seen in all other cockatiel varieties. The White-face does not carry any yellow pigment; without the yellow, the melanin produces a sooty charcoal color. Although both sexes look the same before the first molt, being entirely gray on the head, afterwards the face of the male becomes white. Since the White-face lacks all yellow, it can be easily distinguished from other varieties at a very young age: it has white down. While the female retains the barring underneath the tail and wing feathers, the bars are black and white.

Finally, there is the true albino cockatiel. In this variety all color is lacking. It is becoming a very popular variety and is readily available on the market.

The yellow-face is probably the most recent variety to occur and little to no information is available on it.

SELECTING FOR HEALTH

You may have decided by now which cockatiel variety appeals to you most, and you may be eager to hurry out and find one. Before you do, though, allow yourself sufficent time—time to read a bit more about these charming birds, time to look over a representative number of birds, and time to figure out why you are going to buy a bird in the first place. Selection of a cockatiel is best accomplished by an informed individual. The second point is often overlooked, particularly by a person purchasing his first bird. Once you have found a cockatiel of interest to you, wait! By all means indicate your interest to the salesperson who has shown you the bird and let him know that you will come back to see the bird again. The idea is to view the bird at least two or three times, if at all possible. In this way you are able to

The cockatiel is truly a rewarding pet. Most birds easily win the hearts of many admirers with their beauty and charm.

COCKATIELS AS PETS

No two pied birds are marked the same way. Although the pied cockatiel was the first mutation to occur, it is still considered rare. The demand for this uniquely colored cockatiel has increased greatly.

The health of your bird will be evident in its actions, carriage and appearance. This cinnamon pearl looks to be in fine health.

ensure that you will be buying an alert, healthy bird. By visiting the bird on more than one occasion, you are more likely to detect any abnormalities in its behavior or health.

Choosing a healthy bird is not always a simple matter. There are a number of indicators of good health you should be aware of. In selecting a bird, look for an alert, inquisitive appearance. The eyes of a healthy bird are bright and clear; it is sleek and tight feathered. Only a bird that gives an appearance of well-being should be a candidate for purchase. A bird that spends most of its time with its feathers fluffed up, its eyes closed or swollen, shows discharge from its nostrils, or has a soiled vent should not be considered.

The plumage should be smooth, and the bird should have no bare spots. Broken feathers will grow back in time, so you should not be concerned about them.

Its eyes should be open most of the time and free of any discharge or swelling. Birds that constantly scratch at their eyes, hold one eye closed or have a swelling around an eye probably have an eye problem that is just beginning to develop; they should not be considered.

The nasal openings should be neither clogged nor runny, and there should be no growths on the horny areas of the beak, the cere, or elsewhere. Breathing should be quiet and steady. Labored, noisy, or irregular breathing may be an indicator of respiratory distress.

Should you see a bird you like, ask to have it removed from the cage. While the bird is being held, check its vent

COCKATIELS AS PETS

The best way to keep your cockatiel healthy and safe is to prevent accidents and illness by offering safe, clean surroundings.

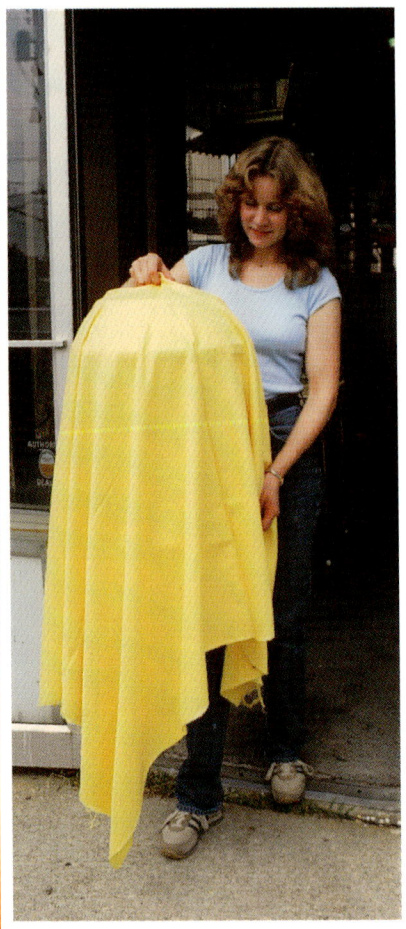

The establishment from where you purchase your cockatiel should be clean, staffed with knowledgeable people and have healthy stock.

for stains and feel the breast to be sure it is not underweight. The breastbone should not protrude. At the same time make sure there are no sores or wounds anywhere on its body.

If you find that the cockatiel you've chosen is suitable, you should now come to a clear agreement with the seller about guarantees. While some dealers will guarantee health, allow exchanges, or refund the purchase price, others do not feel that they can do so—just as you may not be prepared to guarantee that you won't be ill a week from today. But no matter what the laws or policies are that prevail in your area, this is the time to find out about them.

Since you may not feel confident about handling your cockatiel, it is suggested that you ask the seller to do certain tasks for you. You will want your cockatiel to be free of any external parasites when you take it home; ask the seller to ensure this. If the cockatiel's claws need trimming, watch the seller to see how it's done. To facilitate taming, as you'll read later on, it is recommended that the cockatiel's wing feathers be trimmed. Again, watching an experienced person do this will give you confidence if you wish to trim the feathers again, after they are molted.

BRINGING YOUR PET HOME

Though you've made your purchase, you should not take your cockatiel home immediately, unless you've already set up a cage and have everything ready.

It's best to bring your new cockatiel home early in the day, so it will have as much time as possible to become acquainted with its new surroundings. The bird should be carried home in a cardboard box having air holes in its sides. If the day is cool, keep it warm while it's being transported, to safeguard it against becoming chilled. It is not advisable to transport a bird in the rain, not even in a covered box, because of the possibility that it may catch cold.

What you should do first with the cockatiel when you arrive home will depend on how it has reacted to being transported. The pros and cons of beginning taming at once are taken up in a later chapter. Just be certain that you watch the bird's behavior closely from the time you take it from the transport box. In any case, apart from definite taming sessions, for the first few days the cockatiel should not be constantly disturbed. Allow it suffficient opportunity to settle into its cage and new environment.

To make the transition from place to place easier, make sure that the bird is warm enough for the first few days—the room where the cage has been placed should be as warm as the space in which the bird was housed previously. An important way to ease the transition is to bring home some of the seed mix the cockatiel has been used to eating.

Try to make your cockatiel's adjustment to his new home as easy and stress free as possible.

FEEDING AND HOUSING

Do not clutter your cockatiel's cage with too many toys. Your bird will need empty space to exercise and move about in.

One of the special advantages of cockatiels as pets is the ease of feeding them. Their requirements are few and simple, making them easy to keep. Healthy cockatiels are rarely a problem to feed. Like other pet animals, they will do best if given a varied and balanced diet. To prevent problems from arising, feed only recommended foods.

SEED MIXTURES

In the wild, seeds of a number of different grasses are the principal food of cockatiels. Thus the basis for the daily diet of those kept in captivity is a seed mixture prepared specifically for cockatiels. Only such seed mixtures should be used. The basic seed mixture mostly includes millets, oats, and sunflower seeds as the chief ingredients, usually.

One will find different kinds of cockatiel seed mixes on the market. In addition to the brand-name products packaged by a number of large companies, many pet shops and bird specialty stores sell "house mixtures."

For the keeper of a single bird, it is best to purchase fresh seed in small quantities, lest it become stale or spoil. An easy method of testing the freshness of seeds is to place a small amount of seed in a shallow dish after having moistened it thoroughly. If the seed mixture is fresh and you have not allowed it to dry out, more than fifty percent of the seed should sprout in a few days.

Although it may be necessary to sprinkle seed on the bottom of the cage at first, until your new cockatiel has found and begun to take food from the seed cup, placing the seed mixture in the cup only is preferred.

Most of the seed supplied to cockatiels is unhulled. You'll notice that the bird eats the kernel but discards the hull. When you check the seed cup, make sure you don't mistake the hulls that may be in there for uneaten seed. Many people not familiar with keeping birds have made this mistake, and the bird starved to death.

It's worthwhile to get an idea of how much seed your cockatiel usually eats each

If you want to know what your bird is eating, read the ingredient list on the package. If it's all-natural and all-nutritious, it's available to you. Photo courtesy of Noah's Kingdom. Call 1-800-662-4711 for the location of the of the dealer nearest you.

FEEDING AND HOUSING

Bright eyes and clear nostrils are two signs that a cockatiel is in good health.

day. If you know what its normal eating habits are, you will notice immediately if it starts to eat less, perhaps because of illness. You will also be able to leave your bird alone for a long weekend, secure that you have left ample seed in the cage. (This same advice applies to water, too.)

FRUITS AND VEGETABLES

The average bird keeper may not realize the benefits of feeding fruits and vegetables. The vitamin and mineral content of these foods makes them an essential part of your bird's diet. They are necessary for maintaining prime condition, giving your cockatiel its bright eyes and sleek appearance. A cockatiel should be given a portion of fruits or vegetables daily if it is to remain in healthy condition throughout the year. The bird eats wild greens such as chickweed, shepherd's purse, plantain, dandelion, and foxtail. These foods are often not readily available, but it will enjoy many which are, such as spinach, cabbage hearts, brussels sprouts, watercress, and carrot tops. Apple and pear are usually the favorite fruits. Unripened sunflower seeds from one's own garden may be offered too; in fact, a cockatiel is particularly partial to them.

Feed only as much as the bird will eat in a few hours, then remove any leftovers. Vegetables and fruits must not be allowed to wilt and become dirty on the floor of the cage. They should be given to the bird only when fresh. It is essential that all vegetables and fruits be thoroughly washed in warm water to remove any trace of pesticides; even a small amount left on these foods can be fatal. When you first feed fruits or vegetables, your cockatiel may not seem to be interested, probably because it is not accustomed to them. If you continue to offer some each day, your bird will eventually become curious and try them. After a few nibbles, it will eat them each day.

Akin to feeding fruits and vegetables is the practice of offering soaked or sprouted seeds. While the benefits of this are most directly related to breeding pairs of cockatiels, there's no reason not to feed the seed you've sprouted to test the freshness of the mix. If you enjoy sprouted grains in your own meals, your bird will surely relish some too.

The diet of cockatiels in the wild consists mostly of seed, however, not only the ripe, harvested seed found in the cockatiel mix you will be buying. Wild cockatiels have access to seeds in various stages of ripeness, and other vegetable matter as well, depending on the locale and the season. The bird owner can hope only to approximate this state of affairs, particularly since the cockatiel is prevented from searching out the food it may need. In practice, though, the basic daily diet of seed mix accompanied by a variety of fruits and vegetables has proved successful.

Considering the success of the species as a whole, it's obvious that wild cockatiels

Birds have unique dietary needs that must be met by certain seeds and other foods. To be sure your bird is getting what it needs, it's important to feed a diet you can be sure has been created specifically for it by teams of experts. Photo courtesy of Kaytee Products, Inc.

Cockatiels are amusing birds that will surprise you with their antics.

are able to regulate their diet themselves; however, it's reasonable to suppose that some individuals do a better job of this than others. Thus you should be wary of trusting your pet cockatiel to eat only what it needs. It's more often the case that pet parrots eat too much of their favorite foods. It may happen, for example, that your cockatiel will want to eat sunflower seed exclusively, and become too fat.

In this connection let's consider other foods you might offer. Spray millet is usually enjoyed immensely. Tugging the seeds out of the head provides activity as well as food. This is similar to many "treats" made especially for cockatiels, which are mostly seeds held together with some kind of binder. Remember, though, that treats should be used as the name implies, sparingly. Treat foods should be only a small part of a cockatiel's daily food intake. Cheese, most likely a cheddar, is also relished by many cockatiels. It is a good source of calcium, which brings up another aspect of a cockatiel's diet: minerals.

MINERALS

Because of the importance of calcium in the growth of feathers and bone, it is recommended that a cuttlebone always be in your cockatiel's cage. Chewing on the cuttlebone provides activity and helps keep the cockatiel's beak trim. Also available are mineral blocks. The better of these are manufactured to include small amounts of other minerals besides the primary component, calcium.

This need for minerals is recognized in another product prepared for birds, called "grit." Grit is a combination of digestively insoluble particles of gravel and other particles, such as crushed oyster shell, charcoal, mineral salts, and the like, all of which yield their mineral content in the course of digestion.

At present, the practice of offering gravel (and therefore grit) to cage birds is controversial, because gravel has lately been implicated in digestive illnesses. The complicated questions involved will not soon be resolved. However, it can be said that here and there cockatiels are now living apparently healthy lives, both with access to gravel and without it. But while it's uncertain whether the insoluble particles we call gravel are beneficial to a bird's digestion, there is no question about the necessity of minerals. Your cockatiel does require these, in whatever forms they are offered: cuttlebone, mineral blocks) completely digestible grit, or powdered mineral supplements.

Besides mineral supplements, other products are designed to provide vitamins and amino acids,

Millet spray is a well liked treat that many cockatiels eat with relish. Be certain to only offer this once a week otherwise your cockatiel will ignore his beneficial diet for this treat.

Due to the stress of moving, your new pet cockatiel may not eat the first night you have it home. Have food and water available and easily accessible for it anyway.

Although cockatiels come in many different color varieties, choosing one as a pet is truly a matter of personal preference.

FEEDING AND HOUSING

You can trust your bird's diet to a thoroughly researched and quality-tested food that will intensify plumage colors and increase vitality. Photo courtesy of Roudybush, Inc. For more information call (888) 294-2473

while still others combine all three. Oils, such as cod liver oil and wheat germ oil, are primarily seen as sources of vitamins. It is important to remember that dietary supplements are indeed supplements. They may or may not be needed by your cockatiel, depending on a variety of factors: what is provided in the basic daily diet, the environment in which it lives and the amount of exercise it gets, and, finally, the bird's own constitution and food preferences. The considerations that figure in your cockatiel's diet are every bit as complicated as those that determine how you regulate your own diet.

As you've heard, a diet that is varied has the best chance of being nutritionally balanced. Hence it has been recommended that you offer your cockatiel a variety of foods. There is another approach to providing a balanced diet, however, the use of food pellets. Owners of dogs and cats have long been familiar with "dry foods"; the same sort of thing has lately become available for seed-eating birds. The convenience of feeding your cockatiel pellets is obvious, so it may be worthwhile to undertake the task of accustoming your bird to what will most likely be unfamiliar food. Keep in mind that a diet of pellets, like any other diet, must always be monitored. It can happen that a cockatiel, like any other living organism, will need to have its diet adjusted from time to time, depending on circumstances.

One event that is often mentioned in this connection is the molt. As the annual replacement of feathers can be physically stressful for

FEEDING AND HOUSING

When housing several cockatiels in the same cage be sure to supply enough food so that each one has enough to eat.

your cockatiel, it is a time to be particularly careful that the bird's diet is ample—not different, just ample.

WATER

Although cockatiels do not drink a great deal of water, it is important that they always have access to a fresh supply. The water container should be kept scrupulously clean. Fresh water should be given once a day, and the water container should be cleaned thoroughly each time fresh water is provided.

Besides a container for water, two or three other dishes to hold food will be necessary.

CAGE LOCATION

Before you decide to purchase your cockatiel and bring him home, everything necessary for the bird's comfort and health should have been acquired. Your pet's home should be ready and waiting, the cage selected, purchased, and set up. If you fail to do this in advance, you may find yourself trying to fit a stubborn perch in the cage, wondering where to locate the water font and food cups, or discovering that the cage won't fit where you thought it would and having to find another place for it. Should your preparations not be complete when the cockatiel arrives, it will have to remain

An assortment of fresh vegetables will help keep cockatiels looking and feeling their best, and peppers add zest to the variety. Photo courtesy of Eight In One Pet Products, Inc. For more information call (516) 232-1200.

in its small transport box—not that this will cause harm, but it will be much better if any problems relating to the cage set-up and its location have been worked out in advance.

An early consideration should be the location of the cage. Ideally, one should choose a room often frequented by the bird's keeper and other people, since cockatiels are very sociable birds. The bird's home should be placed where it will receive attention; a room where the family often congregates is preferred to a bedroom. A great deal of thought should be given to the placement of the cage because a bird's environment is very important to its continued health and well being. Cockatiels, like most birds, are easily frightened, so they must be given the opportunity to see when people are approaching. The best height for a cage is at eye level, since birds may feel threatened by any movement from above. This is because birds of prey usually approach from above, and your pet will instinctively fear such movements. The cage should be kept in a location free of drafts. Other hazards are fumes of any type, dry air, smoky areas, and high room temperatures. Cockatiels also need to be in a well-lit spot. However, they must not be exposed to bright sunlight for any length of time. Sudden fluctuations in room temperature should also be avoided. As a general rule, if you are comfortable in a given location, your cockatiel will be also. A good place for a cage would be one where there is plenty of light, no drafts, and where the bird is able to observe activity around it.

CAGE DESIGN

A number of considerations go into selecting an appropriate cage, so the matter should be given careful thought. Since cockatiels are hardy birds having a normal life expectancy of more than a decade, a small amount of

Your cockatiel's mirror image will fascinate him and keep him entertained for hours.

time spent choosing the cage will be a worthwhile investment. Visits to pet shops will verify that there are many different cages to choose from. Only a few models are really functional and meet the needs of their prospective occupants. Your pet dealer can often give sensible advice about the advantages and disadvantages of the many cage designs that are on the market. Since you will find cages in all manner of styles, materials, and prices, it's best to consider your choice from a practical viewpoint. This means practical not only from your point of view, but also from that of the cockatiel.

A number of cages are immediately appealing; you think they would look nice with a bird inside, or they would fit in with your decor, however, some of these cages

When purchasing your cockatiel think of where the bird's cage will be located once it is home. An area that is very noisy or that is heavily traveled is not advised.

FEEDING AND HOUSING

Cockatiels are very affectionate pets with much to offer their owners. Like many parrot-like birds, cockatiels have very outgoing personalities.

FEEDING AND HOUSING

Your cockatiel will appreciate time away from the cage to exercise and play. This cockatiel has his own little play gym equipped with toys and ladders.

If you allow your cockatiels out of their cage to free fly for exercise, be careful of what they may get into. Damage to woodwork and to crafts can be substantial.

Play gyms are available from your local pet shop in a wide selection of sizes. Be certain to obtain one that is suitable for cockatiels, as those constructed for budgies may be too small.

do not make good enclosures for a cockatiel, and some will become an annoyance to you because they're so difficult to clean. Happily, there are enough cages attractively designed that will suit both the cockatiel and its keeper for a long while.

Consider the cage from the cockatiel's point of view. In time, the bird will come to regard the cage as its home, its territory. A cockatiel that spends most of its life in a cage must have ample opportunity for exercise, and it will often be eager to leave the cage for movement and companionship. Eventually, the bird will want to return—to eat, nap, or just to be in a place where it feels secure. This "homing" behavior may prove to be helpful once your cockatiel has become tame. For example: you will probably decide the bird should be allowed to fly around the room. When a bird recognizes its cage as home, only a little effort is usually suffficient to encourage the bird to return to it. This sense of home is easily reinforced by feeding it only in its cage. It is also wise to keep your hands out of the cage as much as possible. The idea is to foster the bird's sense that the cage belongs to it alone.

When considering the size of the cage one should remember that cockatiels are powerful fliers and creatures native to wide open spaces; therefore, they should have a roomy cage. The size recommended for larger parrots is preferred. Generally, larger cages are more expensive, but they're better. On the other hand, a bird that will be allowed out of its cage a good deal of the time can do with a smaller one. The main reason to purchase the largest cage you can afford is to ensure that the bird gets enough exercise to keep it healthy. Exercise is important to a bird having to spend most of its time in a relatively small cage. Your cockatiel's cage should be large enough to allow it to stand straight, extend its wings, and stretch, without any part of its body touching the cage. If the cage is not of adequate size, wing and tail feathers will constantly brush against the sides of the cage or stick out

Because of their large wing span, cockatiels need plenty of open space to exercise. Most cages do not offer the birds enough room within the cage and therefore the bird must be allowed freedom.

It is normal for a bird not to play with a toy when it is first introduced into the cage. Cockatiels are a bit leery of new objects, but once accustomed, they quickly become favorites.

cage that is too small for it. Cockatiels are active birds that will make use of all the space you provide for them.

The over-all shape of the cage hasn't been discussed so far. It seems that many people find round cages attractive and decorative. But it's not so obvious that the birds that live inside do. The tall cylindrical cages seem to have little to recommend them for cockatiels. Many bird keepers have concluded that birds prefer rectangular cages. Your cockatiel will probably be happier in a rectangular enclosure in a corner of the room, a bit more snug and cozy than it might be otherwise. Stick to simple shapes and designs. If the sides of the cage extend beyond the base, you can expect feathers, droppings, and seed to be spread over a wider area.

It goes without saying that

The cockatiel is a very active bird that enjoys chewing and pecking on a variety of substances. Give your cockatiel plenty of chew toys or else he will find one of his own!

between the bars. Frayed and damaged feathers, or a dirty, bedraggled bird will be the result of placing your pet in a

a better-built but more expensive cage will be a better investment than a cheaper one. Another reason to evaluate durability is the fact that cockatiels like to chew. Thus, a cage with wooden bars is decidedly impractical. Since cockatiels enjoy chewing and gnawing, give them toys to gnaw on.

The ideal cage for a pet cockatiel is all metal, or plastic and metal. Standard heavy parrot wire is preferred to the thinner wire used for budgerigar cages. Most wire cages available today are plated, not painted, which is good, since paint will chip and the cockatiel may gnaw at it. Additionally, most wire cages are easy to clean and should give many years of service. Construction materials to be avoided are wood, including bamboo and wicker. While these materials may be quite attractive, they are entirely

Cockatiels enjoy the companionship of birds and of humans. If you are unable to be home all day, provide plenty of toys for your pet's enjoyment.

FEEDING AND HOUSING

impractical for cockatiels that will gnaw upon soft woods and thoroughly enjoy doing so.

In choosing a wire cage it's better if the wiring is horizontal rather than vertical, on at least two sides of the cage. Horizontal wiring will allow the cockatiel to climb around more easily. While it's true that cockatiels are able to lead healthy lives in cages with vertical wiring, it may be a bit more difficult for them to climb around. Horizontal wiring may encourage your bird to exercise.

If the cage has horizontal wiring, vertical wires, or both, it's a good idea to be sure the bird's head will not fit between the bars. If it is able to force its head between the bars, the bird may strangle itself.

Now consider the base of the cage. Old-fashioned cages have very shallow bases, sometimes only an inch high. Certainly they let you see everything the bird might be doing, but in time this seems less important in view of the effort required to keep the area around the cage clean of seed hulls and feathers. Newer cages were designed with shallow bases but with panes of glass (later, plastic) fitted along the wire sides. These "seed guards" were something else to clean, and the glass ones got broken now and then. Today, the current trend in cage design is to have a deep base, thereby eliminating the need for seed guards. If you're starting to worry about this, or if you're one of those people who dislike messes so much that neither deep bases nor seed guards will be enough, your pet shop has strips of clear plastic available—again called seed guards—that will wrap around almost any cage.

The bases of most cages you are likely to find incorporate a removable tray. Some trays are shallow, some deep. While the deeper trays may be preferred, one argument in favor of the shallow tray is that it mandates frequent emptying and cleaning, which is all to the good as far as the cockatiel is concerned.

Another feature to be considered is the cage door. The preferred door will have a double catch—one to fasten it open and one to securely fasten it closed—so that your inquisitive pet will not learn to pop it open with its beak. The opening should be large enough for the bird to pass through it easily, and there should be adequate space for your hand to reach inside to perform the necessary chores. All too often a prospective cockatiel owner purchases an oversize budgerigar cage thinking that his bird will have adequate space, only to find the opening in the cage too small for the larger bird.

The door should be constructed so that it will remain open while the bird is out of the cage, in the event it wants to return. A nice feature is a door that is hinged on the bottom; when open it becomes a landing perch, making it easy for your cockatiel to return to the cage.

FURNISHING THE CAGE

The arrangement of the cage is almost as important as its construction. It must be

When choosing a substrate for your pet's enclosure, look for a material that's resilient to molding, dust-free, biodegradable and all-natural. With all these features, your pets will be kept clean and dry. Photo courtesy of Northeastern Products.

easy to clean; both you and the bird should be able to reach the seed and water containers with ease. There should be at least three perches, and the cage design should provide enough flexibility to arrange them in a hygienic fashion. Positioning of the perches is important; they should not be placed in locations where the bird's droppings can foul the food or water. This is an essential of cage arrangement. Perches should allow easy access to food and water, and one should be near the top of the cage.

It is best that the perches be of different diameters so that the bird's grasp will vary. If at all possible, the perches that come with the cage should be replaced with natural branches, from fruit, elm, hazelnut, willow, alder, or hawthorn trees, for example. This will not only make for perches of varying diameters but will also provide something for the bird to gnaw on. It should be noted that a cockatiel's feet are considerably larger than those of a canary or budgerigar; consequently their perches should be about an inch in diameter. Constant nibbling by the cockatiel as well as scraping and cleaning by the owner necessitate somewhat frequent replacement of the perches.

There are a number of other aspects to be considered when picking out a cage for your cockatiel. It might not be possible to find the ideal cage, but the closer you can come to finding all of the desirable features, the easier will be your job of caring for the bird.

Some manufacturers equip their cages with fitted food cups that can be serviced from outside the cage. While this is a handy feature, it is not too important, as other types of food cups can be located anywhere in the cage without limiting your cage arrangement. If accessories supplied with the cage, such as perches and seed cups, do not meet your needs or those of the bird, substitute items are available. The substitutes may be more easily cleaned, installed, or filled. You may wish to consider installation of a tube drinker. While a slight additional expense is involved, most owners feel the convenience to be well worth it. Tube drinkers are not fouled as easily as open water cups, and they hold a larger supply. While it's still best to change the water daily, the larger capacity will allow you to leave your cockatiel unattended for a couple of days.

A modern, well-stocked pet shop may display an unbelievable array of attractive accessories, toys, and other items for the comfort and joy of your bird. It is often difficult, even irresistible, to avoid the temptation to purchase more than one needs. The only items initially essential are perches, food and water vessels, and a cuttlebone. After your bird has settled into its new home, you may wish to acquire some well constructed toys to provide both enjoyment and exercise for your pet.

When purchasing a cage, think about a cover for it. It is not an absolute necessity, but a cover may be useful. Cockatiels do not see well in the dark and often become startled or frightened at strange sounds. It is best to completely cover a cage at night to avoid having the bird thrash around in the cage and injure itself. Covers also keep the bird cozy and free from subtle drafts while it's sleeping. Quiet and darkness are more conducive to sleep. The bird soon learns that when the cover is on, it is bedtime, and it will settle down for the night. Cage covers are also useful in quieting the bird, as some birds can become quite annoying with their constant chattering or talking.

These beautiful cockatiels are of the pearled variety. Many new cockatiel mutations are becoming popular as more people are breeding these birds as a hobby.

COCKATIEL CARE

Whenever you are thinking of purchasing something for your cockatiel, whether it be the cage, a toy, or a food treat, be certain to evaluate it for safety, just as you would something that will be used by a child. Some bird toys have metal or plastic parts that will not stand up to a cockatiel's beak. Cockatiels have been injured by toys they've been able to tear apart.

PREVENTING ACCIDENTS

When you are ready to allow your cockatiel outside its cage, remember to consider the mischief it may get into. A bird should not be allowed the freedom of a room unless someone is there to watch it. For example, doors and windows should be closed. Windows can be treacherous: your cockatiel may be unfamiliar with them and try to fly on through. Be sure to remove anything you think may be dangerous to your pet.

It is generally agreed that their natural curiosity makes cockatiels somewhat accident-prone. If your bird is to be allowed any degree of freedom out of its cage, a great deal of care must be taken to ensure a safe environment. More often than not, the owner of a cockatiel is at fault when there is an unfortunate mishap. It's the owner's responsibility to foresee the danger to the bird and take the necessary steps to prevent an accident. The kinds of trouble a bird can get into are unbelievable; it takes a great deal of foresight and imagination to prevent your pet from harming itself. Cockatiels, like small children, should never be allowed their freedom without giving thought to hazards that

Many household plants are poisonous to your cockatiel if he should nibble on them. Always monitor your bird when he is out of his cage so that an unfortunate accident does not occur.

COCKATIEL CARE

Cockatiels are the most affectionate and easily tamed of the smaller parrot-like birds. They prefer to cuddle with their owner rather than be rough housed.

may be present. They should never be left unsupervised for even a short time.

Can you imagine a cockatiel drowning in a pitcher of water, being shut inside a refrigerator, being caught by a pet cat, or flying into a mirror and breaking its neck? Stranger accidents than these have happened to cockatiels, and they can happen to your bird if you are not careful when the bird is allowed some freedom. The age-old phrase, "An ounce of prevention is worth a pound of cure," is most appropriate here.

PREVENTING ILLNESS

As with accidents, illness is best dealt with in terms of prevention. So far as infectious diseases are concerned, the key to prevention is cleanliness. The bird's surroundings—cage and play area—should be kept scrupulously clean. Generally, cockatiels are tidy birds, so cleaning up after them is not much of a problem. It takes only a few moments to do the job, and your bird certainly deserves a clean environment. It is best to clean the cage each day, either in the morning or the evening. Cleaning every other day is an absolute minimum. The cage tray should be cleaned and the paper liner removed and replaced. A regular cleaning schedule must be maintained, not only for the tray but also for the perches, food and water containers, toys, playground, and the cage cover. The water font should be cleansed daily, while the other parts of the cage and objects in and around it should receive attention once a week.

On a monthly basis everything should be thoroughly cleaned. The scrubbing should be done with hot water containing a strong disinfectant, followed by hot and cold water rinses. After being cleaned, all items must be carefully dried. Perches may be either washed or scraped; if washed, let them dry completely before putting them back in the cage.

BATHING

Washing is fine for the cage and accessories, and it's good for your cockatiel too. It's best if the cockatiel does it itself, if it takes baths regularly.

Although cockatiels originate in open, semi-arid regions, they have been observed bathing and splashing about on the edges of small pools in stream beds. In the wild, they are naturally "bathed" by rain showers, so they seem to particularly enjoy being showered by falling spray or rain. When the bird preens, you will see that it occasionally obtains a bit of oil from a gland located near the base of the tail. The oil is rubbed over the feathers by the beak.

To provide your bird with an opportunity to bathe, a shallow bowl, heavy enough to prevent accidental tipping, can be used for a bird bath. Those made of red clay,

Be sure any wild or outside grown plant that you give to your cockatiel is safe and non-toxic.

COCKATIEL CARE

available from garden and pet shops, are ideal. It is not necessary to leave the bowl in the cage at all times; it can be placed in the cage every few days for about a half hour. Room temperature water should be used in the bath.

We do not advocate the often-mentioned practice of allowing your bird to bathe or shower in the kitchen sink. Even though cockatiels seem to naturally gravitate to a running faucet and attempt to shower underneath it, once they learn to do this, there is the possibility they will attempt to steal a bath when the water is unusually hot and thus be tragically killed.

Alternatively, you may want to try spraying your cockatiel with room temperature water. Garden sprayers used for misting plants are ideal for this purpose. One should spray with caution as some birds may be frightened by the spray until they become used to it. Baths serve to stimulate preening and improve the appearance of the plumage.

Throughout this book, suggestions have been given to help you to know about the essentials of cockatiel care. The described regimen, recommendations about cleanliness, and comments regarding feeding have not been casually suggested—they are *absolutely essential* if you are to maintain a healthy bird. When a cockatiel is well fed on a balanced diet of fresh, nutritional foods; when it has been housed in a sanitary environment that is maintained with a carefully followed cleaning schedule; when it is kept free of dampness, drafts, and other harmful conditions in the area where it is housed; and when given sufficient exercise, you will find it is likely to suffer from very few ailments. Under such conditions, in fact,

Your cockatiel will enjoy all the attention he can get. A tame bird will enjoy eating from your hand.

The cockatiel does not generally utilize his foot as a hand for holding food as do many hookbills. When he occasionally does, he lacks the dexterity that other parrots possess.

illness is a rare occurrence. It is far better to avoid sickness by keeping a bird under optimal living conditions than to try to cure it once it has become ill. Furthermore, it is not always possible to cure an ailing bird; this is particularly true if the ailment is either incorrectly diagnosed or recognized too late for treatment to be effective.

FIRST AID

Whether your cockatiel has an accident or becomes ill, immediate, correct treatment is essential. Although there are a few relatively simple health problems that can be dealt with, and in spite of the fact that there are some first-aid measures that are generally beneficial, the safest and most advisable course of action is to consult an experienced veterinarian. Since veterinary physicians experienced in the treatment of birds are sometimes difficult to find, you may wish to seek one out in advance. This should be done while

Oftentimes, housing more than one bird in a cage can prove hazardous. Two birds usually fare well together, however, a third party can cause an unfriendly upset and fighting may occur.

your bird is still healthy—the "ounce of prevention" again.

Since it's not possible to adequately cover all the problems that may afflict a pet cockatiel, only some first-aid measures will be discussed. To further prepare yourself for eventualities, it is recommended that you read one of the books available on this aspect of bird care.

Accidents often result in bleeding. In all cases, it's imperative to stop the bleeding at once. Styptic powder and pressure will usually do the job. If bleeding persists, or if the wound is so large as to require suturing, or if healing is not apparent in a few days, then veterinary attention is necessary.

Another frequent result of accidents is a broken bone. The important thing is to immobilize the bird, by wrapping it in a towel, for example, to prevent further damage. Professional help offers the best chance of successfully repairing the fracture and averting lameness.

Burns should be flushed with cold water, then dried gently. If your cockatiel has been exposed to toxic fumes, remove the bird to fresh air immediately. The correct response to poisoning depends on what the poison is; call your veterinarian or local poison-control center immediately.

Any of the foregoing, as well as other trauma, may cause your cockatiel to go into shock. If your bird is immobile, breathing rapidly, with feathers fluffed, you should suspect shock. It is imperative to conserve the bird's body heat until you can get veterinary attention. Wrap it in a towel, cover the cage, or use a heat lamp. Be careful not to change the bird's position abruptly, as this may cause death. Remember, shock is serious. Careful, gentle handling of ill or injured birds is mandatory, as shock or its aggravation is

Your new pet cockatiel will have to become familiar with his new surroundings. It would be a good idea for you to be present during his first days of exploring.

always possible.

Injuries resulting from accidents have one good feature: they are usually easy to spot. More insidious are diseases that have a slow and subtle onset. Birds may in fact be ill long before they show it; the only way to deal with this is to observe your cockatiel daily, to be sure you don't miss the earliest signs of illness. You should quickly recognize that something is amiss should the bird exhibit ruffled feathers, loss of appetite, listlessness, excessive thirst, discharge from the eyes and nostrils, watery and discolored droppings, or other more obvious signs of illness. Generally speaking, the puffed, huddled, sick appearance is obvious and easily recognized. A sick bird will often sleep with both feet widely spread on the perch;

Before you allow your bird to fly free throughout the house, be sure that it is familiar with doors and windows so that it does not injure itself by flying into or out of one.

resting on one foot with the other drawn up, on the other hand, is a sign of good health. Closing eyelids is another danger signal.

If your cockatiel shows any of these signs, the first step is to warm it. Depending on the cage, the temperature inside can be increased by covering it with a towel and placing it on a heating pad. Heat lamps and ordinary incandescent light bulbs can also be used, though less successfully. The temperature inside the cage should be kept between 85-90° F. Some improvement should be noted within a few hours. During this time, be careful to notice whether your cockatiel is eating normally. If you do not find evident improvement in the bird's condition by the next day, it's time to consult your vet.

On the whole, bird diseases tend to progress rapidly. This has to do with your cockatiel's small size and high rate of metabolism. If you value your pet, it is best to seek professional help immediately when illness occurs. It's too often the case that stop-gap home remedies are beside the point and only make treatment specific to the illness more diffficult when it is undertaken—if it isn't by then too late.

You can take courage from the fact that a cockatiel kept alone is not exposed to the main avenue of disease: other birds. There is only a slight chance that illness can be introduced via food or supplies. If a few months have passed since you acquired your cockatiel and it appears as healthy as ever, you can look forward to an illness-free future.

This consideration applies as well to parasites, such as mites and lice. If the cockatiel you purchase is free of them, it will not get them

It is easier to handle your pet cockatiel if his wing is trimmed. Do not attempt to do this yourself, however, take him to your veterinarian and have him show you how it should be done.

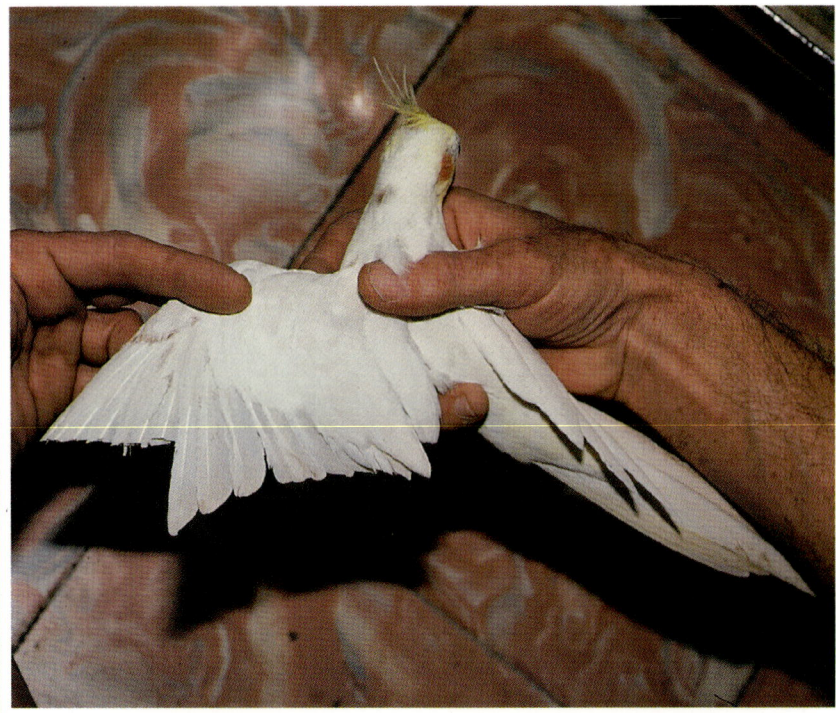

> Cockatiels do not have the brilliancy of coloration as most other parrots; they have a subdued beauty all their own.

If you are concerned that your pet cockatiel may have mites, thoroughly clean the cage and all its accessories, and treat your pet with the proper mite or lice powder available at your local pet shop.

spontaneously thereafter. When you purchase your cockatiel, ask the seller to make sure that it is free of parasites.

Just as you looked your cockatiel over closely when you purchased it, you should do the same whenever you have it in hand for grooming purposes. If you happen to be clipping claws, take the time to give your cockatiel something of a physical examination.

In case you don't recall clearly how the seller handled your cockatiel when you bought it, it may be helpful to describe how a cockatiel may be restrained.

Quick movements are to be avoided. When handling a bird, be as gentle as possible at all times. A cockatiel should be held with the thumb and first finger controlling the head. If the bird attempts to bite you, placing your thumb under the beak will control its movement. When holding the bird in your hand, be sure that you do not restrict respiration. Also, do not press against the nostrils or eyes.

While holding a bird for examination can be done by one person, unless you have a particularly tame bird, two pairs of hands are preferred for trimming. One person holds the bird, watching its respiration and holding it still. The individual holding the bird should neither pull its head nor push it into the body. The bird's body should not be allowed to twist. The bird should be supported on one's lap or on a towel-covered counter. While it is being carefully held, a second person should do the trimming.

It's not strictly necessary to trim the claws of an active cockatiel as normal climbing and perching activity serves to keep them suffficiently worn

Should your cockatiel fall ill, it is wisest to move him away from your other birds so that he does not spread his illness and infect the remaining stock.

Natural perches and tree branches benefit your cockatiel in a number of ways, one of them being keeping the toenails trim by naturally wearing them down.

down. If the claws become too long, they curve back in such a way that the cockatiel will find it diffficult to grip the perch. Specially made bird-claw clippers should be used to snip off the tip of the claw. There is a dark blood vessel along the inside of the claw, that may be seen by holding the claw up to a light source. Be sure to avoid clipping into this blood vessel. Should there be an accident, with resultant bleeding, apply styptic powder with light pressure.

As an active, healthy bird will not have beak problems, trimming the beak is rarely necessary. If a problem with the beak develops, try to determine the cause, instead of just trimming and forgetting that a problem exists. A beak conditioner, cuttlebone, and mineral block will often prevent such difficulties. If your bird should

COCKATIEL CARE

develop a misshapen or overgrown beak it will have to be trimmed back to its normal shape. If this is not done, the bird will have difficulty cracking seeds and may not be able to eat properly. It also becomes almost impossible for the bird to preen its feathers if the beak is deformed. After the beak has been trimmed—with scissors or clippers, whichever is appropriate—the edges can be smoothed with a nail file or emery board. In trimming the beak you are attempting to return it to a natural configuration. The same procedure is followed for both the top and bottom parts of the beak. When the trimming is finished, check to see that the beak closes correctly. As with the claws, the beak contains a blood supply; since this is extensive, extreme care should be taken when cutting. Some bird owners are hesitant to attempt to trim a beak, preferring to engage professional assistance—this is a wise attitude.

Many experts in bird taming advocate trimming the wing feathers to restrict flight. This will prevent the bird from getting away from you, making taming far easier. "Trimming the wings," as it's often called, means cutting only *part* of the wing *feathers*. It's usually necessary to trim the feathers of only one wing, the purpose being to unbalance the cockatiel's flight. With a particularly energetic bird, it may be necessary to trim both wings.

Before starting, look for any "blood feathers"; they should not be clipped. A blood feather, or pin feather, is one that has not finished growing. Part of the feather is still enclosed in its sheath, which has a blood supply. If cut, the sheath may bleed considerably. Should you accidentally cut a blood feather, styptic powder should be applied to stop the bleeding.

Again, it's best to have two persons for this procedure: one to hold and one to clip. The two feathers at the end of the wing are usually left uncut for the sake of appearance. The adjacent ten feathers should at first be cut halfway from wing to tip. If this proves insuffficient, the feathers may be trimmed further, so long as at least one-half inch of feather is left extending from the wing.

A bird's plumage will stay in its optimum condition with plenty of baths. Be sure, however, that he bathes early in the day so that he can dry off well before nighttime and not catch a chill.

TAMING AND TRAINING

Before beginning to outline a program, or schedule, and indicating techniques for taming and training, some general advice is in order. Fundamentally, the taming process boils down to allowing your cockatiel to become accustomed to you.

This means that you alone should be the person doing the taming of your bird. Once the bird has become tame and has gained a great deal of confidence in you, it can be introduced to other members of the family, perhaps even to friends or visitors. In the beginning, however, others in the family should be asked to stay away from it. You will have to explain the reason for this enforced solitude if a family feud is to be avoided. Others who are interested in the bird will have to be told they will have an opportunity to become acquainted with it at a later time. Your bird must become totally tame with you before you can begin to think about its being tame with strangers. The key to all of this is frequent contact—try to spend as much time as possible with your new pet. The more attention you are able to give your cockatiel, the more tame it will become. It is also true that once your bird is tame, if it then has sufficient contact with your family, it will likely be tame with them as well.

WHAT TO EXPECT

There are some clues as to what you can expect of a bird. If a young cockatiel reacts favorably to being handled when you buy it, you can expect that it will be reasonably easy to tame. If you happen to be able to find a cockatiel that already knows a word or two, it is certainly reasonable to expect that the bird's vocabulary can be developed further without much difficulty.

The variety of experiences any bird has had before you obtain it will, without a doubt, influence its behavior. At least to some degree, the cockatiel has begun to form its personality by the time you acquire it. If the bird you have selected behaves calmly while the pet dealer trims its wing feathers and claws, you may rest assured that the bird has already experienced gentle handling by others.

Just as observation of the cockatiel you've chosen will give you an idea of what to hope for from it, so should

Shiny objects are appealing to cockatiels. Always make sure the toys your cockatiel plays with have no sharp edges or pieces that could fall off and injure him.

Your local pet shop should have a large assortment of cockatiels for you to choose from. All birds should be healthy and full of energy as well as have good weight to their body.

TAMING AND TRAINING

observation be the basis for deciding how soon you should begin training your bird. There are two schools of thought about this: one suggests that taming should begin immediately, as soon as you get your cockatiel home; the other believes you should let your bird get accustomed to its new home for a while, perhaps even a few days. The strategy you employ with your cockatiel should be determined by what you are able to tell from its behavior.

Any cockatiel you're likely to obtain has spent its entire life in captivity. It has always been around people, more or less. Thus, human handling will result in little stress, compared to what may be experienced by a wild-caught bird. Similarly, you can expect that your cockatiel will not be severely affected by being moved from one location to another. But it will still take some time for the cockatiel to adjust to its new surroundings. Many bird trainers see an opportunity here; they advise undertaking taming immediately because it seems the bird's disorientation in a new location makes it more amenable to learning. If you wish to follow this course, you should arrange to bring your cockatiel home early enough in the day so that you can have your first taming session as soon as the bird is taken out of the transport box. The first day the bird is at home, spend as much time as you can with it. Watch the bird carefully; if there is any sign of stress, if the bird seems unwell, or if the taming is not proceeding satisfactorily, it's best to put the bird in its cage and wait for another time. Should this happen, you will in effect be forced to follow the second approach mentioned—beginning taming at some later time.

The tame-later approach certainly minimizes any unnecessary stress to the cockatiel, making the transition to a new home as easy as possible. You also have a good opportunity to observe the bird and to be sure it is doing well. There is always the possibility that the cockatiel will have had a difficult time during the trip home.

A FLEXIBLE PROGRAM

In addition to the fact that there are two schools of thought about how soon you should begin taming, there is also a difference of opinion about every other point in training birds. The conclusions that may be reached from all this are clear: there's more than one way to accomplish any training task, and no one way is entirely superior to another. You will have to decide which methods best suit you, and the methods will depend on your ability, your situation, and, most important of all, your cockatiel.

Two cockatiels that are housed together will form a close bond to each other and will not want to be bothered with you. Do not expect to hand tame these birds, but be happy with the companionship that they give.

One of the first ways of taming your cockatiel is to use a perch. This is especially helpful when trying to get your bird down from high places or off of its cage.

There's an encouraging side to this lengthy discussion. No single aspect, in the entire process of taming and training, is critical to its overall success. Just as to start taming later, instead of immediately, does not spell failure, two training sessions a day instead of four does not either. On the other hand, recognize that while no single step is critical to your success, the aggregate is. You won't end up with the kind of performance you want if you find yourself fudging a little every step of the way.

THE TAMING AREA

Taming your cockatiel is the first step to accomplish. All efforts at taming should be conducted in the same, distraction-free area. Taming is best accomplished in a confined area, so the bird cannot get away from you. Thus, it may be possible to tame the bird in its cage, but the success of this approach depends on how wild, or territorial, your cockatiel is and how much space within the cage it has to avoid you. For example, the cockatiel may decide to retreat to a high corner, and you'll have to twist your arm through the door repeatedly in attempts to get your hand—or a taming stick—close to the bird. All things considered, taming will proceed more smoothly if both you and the bird have room to maneuver. For this reason—and the fact that your cockatiel is likely to be more aggressive in what it considers to be its own territory—it is preferable to tame your cockatiel outside its cage. A small room then becomes the choice for a taming area. If it's necessary to conduct the taming sessions in a larger room, you can use some kind of sheet to enclose a convenient corner. The taming area should be a place where you and the bird can move freely, within comfortable limits.

Since your cockatiel will be unable to fly because its feathers are trimmed, it's best to work on the floor. This way the cockatiel is less likely to injure itself. It will take a little time before the bird realizes it can no longer fly. Even then it's possible that it may still launch itself into the air. Feather clipping may not eliminate the problem of chasing the bird around the room, but it's imperative that you keep in mind the danger of falls, so long as the bird is unable to fly.

It is relatively easy to hand tame a cockatiel and once done, your bird will want to be with you all the time.

The use of food rewards will help a great deal in training the cockatiel.

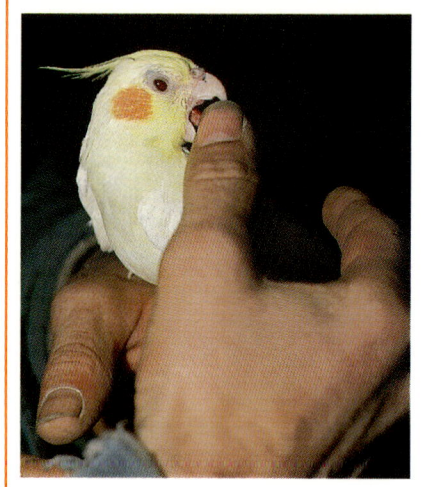

Only one person should initially train the cockatiel. After this, the rest of the family is encouraged to play with the bird as much as possible.

In order to ensure that the attention of the bird is completely focused on you during taming and training, all distractions must be removed from the taming area. Mirrors should be covered or removed. Work with the bird as often as possible, and use short lessons to keep its attention. The more brief sessions you are able to work into your bird's day, the faster it will learn.

SCHEDULING SESSIONS

This brings up the matter of scheduling training sessions. It should be clear to you that training will take a reasonable amount of time. Those who are most successful at it are the ones who are able to spend enough time with their cockatiels to accomplish the task. You already know that frequency of contact with your bird is an all-important factor. It is generally accepted that many short sessions each day will give better results than one or two longer sessions. Each training session should last from 10-15 minutes. Several sessions should be held each day. Repetition is the key to taming a cockatiel.

Even if you are a very busy person, you should schedule a minimum of two sessions with your cockatiel every day, more whenever possible. The more sessions you are able to schedule, the greater the likelihood that you will be successful. The obvious times for taming and training are in the morning and in the evening. As with any other task, the sooner you start to work with your bird, and the harder you work at it, the more likely it is that you will get the desired results. Just remember that the results cannot be guaranteed in advance; there are far too many variables. It is a fact that some cockatiels will become more tame than others; that some will be good performers and others won't; and that some develop relatively large vocabularies, while many do not. These observations serve to underline the fact that every cockatiel is an individual!

A COCKATIEL'S MOODS

You will be much more successful in taming and training if you pay close attention to your cockatiel's moods. A cardinal rule in bird keeping is to *observe the bird.* Try to put yourself into its place and imagine what it is experiencing. While we certainly understand that a cockatiel is not a little human being and cannot be expected to behave as we do, it is most important that we remember that the bird is not a wind-up toy; it deserves attention. As

If you have two cockatiels it is best to tame one bird at a time and then you may work with them at the same time. It is not until each bird is tame, however, that working with them together in this fashion will be possible.

TAMING AND TRAINING

Cockatiels make excellent pets for responsible children.

you work with your bird, keep in mind that its day is pretty much like yours. There are times when it wants to make noise, times when it wants to take a nap, and times when it is physically active. When the cockatiel wants to play with its toys or fly about its play area, these are the times to teach tricks. However, this mood is not compatible with training it to talk.

Although every cockatiel has a wide range of moods, just as humans do, the range will be different from bird to bird. The experiences of a friend with his or her bird may be somewhat different from those you have with your cockatiel. Each bird has its own personality. If you haven't had experience with a number of birds, this won't be obvious; but after looking at a cage full of cockatiels in a pet shop, the variations in activity level will be readily apparent.

In general, the periods when your cockatiel is most excited will not be productive for taming or training. Indeed, you may get better results in taming if you work with your bird when it is in a less active, quieter mood. The bird is likely to be more tractable at these times.

If some of your training or taming sessions should turn out to be failures, there is always the possibility this may have happened because the bird simply wasn't in the right mood for the activity you had in mind.

Besides paying close attention to your cockatiel's behavior, it's also essential that you watch your own. How you behave whenever you are around a bird is important.

OWNER'S BEHAVIOR

From the moment you bring your cockatiel home you are in a position to win its friendship. This does not mean that you are required to begin working with your bird at once. It does mean, however, that everything that happens in the cockatiel's vicinity will have some effect on it. It becomes very important for you to be aware of what you are doing in the presence of your cockatiel.

When working near the bird, make every attempt to move purposefully; quick, unexpected movements may frighten it and delay the formation of the bond you are attempting to foster between the bird and yourself.

When a bird is cupped in your hand and no pressure is being applied, it will not bite you. This actually makes the bird feel more secure.

The way you talk to the bird is also important. It makes little difference to the cockatiel if you are talking to it or to someone across the room. Your voice should always be quiet, gentle, calm, and reassuring.

Taming is nothing more than getting your pet accustomed to you, to climb upon your finger, to allow you to take it in and out of its cage.

HAND TAMING

Almost by definition, when we think of a tame bird, we usually think of a bird that will perch on one's finger. Strictly speaking, such a bird is *hand tame*. Tameness properly understood is a matter of degree. Wild birds are described as tame if they allow you to approach within a few feet before flying away. At the other extreme are cage birds that will allow you to handle their plumage and will lie motionless in your hands. Not all cockatiels will come to permit this sort of handling, so don't be surprised if yours doesn't.

It's worth considering what your hands represent to a bird. It's not the nature of birds to be inclined toward much physical contact. In many species, the mere fact that they press their bodies together while perching seems remarkable enough to deserve comment, since most birds prefer to keep some space between themselves and their fellows. (It's worth noting that if you want something to fondle, you'll be more satisfied with a dog or a cat.) Unless a bird becomes accustomed to human hands during its infancy, its first experience with hands will be as an unwanted restraint. Moreover, even many hand-raised birds, as they mature, will be less inclined to be held.

It is not possible to avoid instances in which a bird will experience hands as a restraint; claw clipping and physical examinations will be necessary from time to time. One way to prevent having the bird make negative associations with your hands is to wear thin gloves on these occasions.

Many people contemplating taming a bird are worried about being bitten. With a cockatiel this is a valid concern, as they can inflict painful bites (although they do little damage). Birds bite because they are frightened or nervous. Biting will become a serious behavior problem if the bird is constantly uncomfortable in its surroundings. If your cockatiel bites, the only response you should make is a loud "no!" If it persists in biting, discontinue the taming session, and wait until the bird is more mellow.

When working with your cockatiel, be careful that you aren't mistaking what the cockatiel may be trying to do

Like all animals, birds love special treats. Owners can feel especially good knowing they're giving their pet birds something that tastes good and is good for them. Photo courtesy of Kaytee Products, Inc.

TAMING AND TRAINING

with its beak. Cockatiels, like other parrots, use their beaks in ways that many other birds do not. Biting is a means of defense, of course, but even a tame cockatiel will at times nibble on your finger. This behavior can be understood because of their inclination to gnaw; they also use their beaks to move about. Notice how your cockatiel employs its beak. Very often, before moving to an unfamiliar perch, a cockatiel will test it with its beak. When you first present a finger to your cockatiel, if it reaches out slowly with an open beak, it's probably trying to determine if your finger is a secure perch. Bites are usually delivered swiftly.

TAMING WITH STICKS

If your cockatiel is inclined to bite, then it is recommended that you begin taming it by using sticks, instead of offering your hand. As with many other aspects of cockatiel taming that have already been noted, there is some question about the use of sticks, whether these be dowels, such as those used for perches, or small branches from trees. Cockatiels are smart enough to know the difference between sticks and hands and to recognize that sticks are held in your hand. Some trainers look upon teaching a cockatiel to step on and off a stick as the first stage in the process of hand-taming. Others believe that stick training is unnecessary and can be eliminated entirely. The latter have obviously not been dissuaded by a painful bite from the cockatiel's strong beak. Stick training is a good

The taming process can go a long way toward establishing a good relationship between you and your pet.

beginning because the cockatiel is accustomed to perching on sticks. Should your bird be one of the wilder ones, taming will probably proceed more smoothly if you start with stick training.

Perhaps a more interesting argument is that training your bird to step onto a stick held by you may prove very useful. For example, if your cockatiel gets itself into a position that is difficult to reach, it is very handy to have the bird step onto a stick so that you can bring it within reach. In any event, it's a good idea to have a t-stick around, for they have many uses. The t-stick consists of two dowels, of an appropriate size, joined together in the shape of the letter T; the handle should be at least two feet long.

THE TAMING PROGRAM

When you're ready to begin the first taming session, move either the transport box or the cage into the taming area. Open the box and the bird will soon come out. If the bird is in its cage, it may venture out if you merely open the door. But if you remove the bottom and turn the cage on its side, this will allow you to approach the bird.

Should the bird react wildly as you approach it, do not jerk away. If you make this mistake, the cockatiel will soon learn how to keep you at bay. With the bird on the floor, take the stick (or your finger) and move it in front of the bird until it touches the bird's abdomen, above and in front of its feet. You are attempting to get the cockatiel to step up onto the stick. You want it to stay perched on the stick as you hold it. If you move the stick, the cockatiel will probably jump off. This is your cue to present the stick again. The cockatiel must be taught to step onto the stick when it is presented, and to stay there. When this has been accomplished, take a second stick and teach the cockatiel to step up from one to another. As you drill the cockatiel in these maneuvers, it becomes more and more accustomed to your being close to it. Other drills can teach the cockatiel to step from the stick to the T-stick, to a playground, or onto or into its cage, as you like. Stick training can be said to be accomplished when the cockatiel will remain quietly perched on the stick as you stand and move about the taming area.

A stick is one thing but your hand is another. The next stage in taming is this: with your cockatiel perched on a stick, present a finger as you did the second stick. Try to have the cockatiel step from the stick onto your finger. If the bird is very reluctant to do this, go back to drills with sticks alone. Try offering food rewards by hand in the course of the drill; this should have the effect of lessening the bird's fear of your hands. Try a sunflower seed; if that doesn't work, try spray millet. A timid cockatiel may be more inclined to nibble the end of a long spray of millet. With time, you can offer shorter and shorter lengths.

In hand taming, many people are amazed to find that their bird will soon step onto their finger and move quickly onto their arm or even their shoulder. "What success!" they think. Actually, the bird may just be making its escape from those treacherous hands. Successful hand taming means that your cockatiel will be content to remain perched on your hand, not on your shoulder. Drill the bird in perching on your hands by having it step from finger to finger.

REPETITION AND REINFORCEMENT

By now the importance of drills in each behavior should be obvious. It's desirable that each be mastered before moving onto the next. Subsequent taming sessions should review what has been taught in the previous ones. You will find that all the ways you can handle your cockatiel will come in handy at one time or another.

Provided your cockatiel is willing to accept food from your hands, rewards do seem to hasten learning. Once a bird has become hand-tame, they can certainly be useful in teaching more complicated tricks.

You may wish to also employ verbal commands in the course of your taming exercises. Though a cockatiel will step onto a stick because it is presented, not because you say "Up," the bird can associate the command with the behavior. By further training, "Up" can eventually be used to cue the cockatiel to hop from a perch to a held stick, for example, or to fly from one to the other.

TEACHING TRICKS

You may be content with the repertoire of tricks your cockatiel is able to teach itself, or you may wish to a take a more active role in its training. You will find that a pet cockatiel, left to its own devices or given an interesting toy, will amaze you with the tricks it can do. A tame cockatiel kept by itself enjoys inventing its own tricks—all the bird needs is a chance to do so. If you want to increase the chances of your cockatiel's keeping itself happily occupied, and at the same time providing you with hours of amusement, go to your local pet shop and pick out a playground. There are a number of designs from which to choose. You will find playgrounds made of metal, wood, or plastic and equipped with swings, perches, ladders, and bells. The variety is almost endless. Purchase a playground that is large enough for a cockatiel; some designed for budgerigars will not accommodate the larger bird. Prices depend on how elaborate the playground is. You are sure to find one that will meet your needs.

Once the playground is placed in an appropriate, and carefully selected location, you will find that it affords a means of keeping your cockatiel interested and occupied. It is often convenient to place the playground near the cage. Whenever the bird is allowed out of the cage, it will probably move to the playground and spend a great deal of time amusing itself there. Some of the unexpected advantages of such a device are that it will keep your cockatiel away from doors and windows and unsafe areas, and it will give the bird a place to perch that is not inconvenient for you. A playground of any type is a worthwhile investment, as it provides endless fun for the bird as well as pleasure for

TAMING AND TRAINING

> The key to trick training your cockatiel is to have him learn something he is naturally inclined to do such as climbing up a ladder.

you.

If you choose a more active role in teaching your cockatiel some tricks, it will be helpful to remember that all tricks are based on three simple acts: riding, climbing, and using the beak. If you can teach your bird to do these three things, you will be repaid with an endless display of variations of these three basic acts.

It is helpful to understand that in spite of the fact that cockatiels are intelligent birds, there is a limit to their ability to learn. There is also the fact that they are quite easily distracted. Since animals learn by association, it is necessary to reward proper performance *immediately so* that the bird comes to realize what is expected or (from the bird's viewpoint) what behavior will result in the reward of a treat. If teaching the trick is to be effective, your cockatiel must learn that the reward comes as a result of its correct behavior.

Teaching tricks can be a tedious job; for some people, it may take over a year to teach the most diffficult tricks. Before you make the decision to engage in teaching some tricks to your cockatiel, be sure that you have the patience and temperament required for the job. Also decide whether the expenditure of time is worth the result. If you think you can do the job, and you want to, go to it!

Climbing a Ladder

Cockatiels enjoy climbing up and down the sides of their cages. It will not take long for your bird to learn to go up a ladder. If you place the cockatiel on the bottom rung, it may just begin to climb by itself. If not, give the bird a gentle push. Keep pushing if the bird hesitates at any step. Don't let the cockatiel jump off or go only halfway up. It should be taught to climb all the way to the top of the ladder each time. Repeat the process over and over again, rewarding your pet each time it is successful. Keep each session short; also, don't attempt to teach more than one trick at a time.

It is very important for the owner to gain trust from his pet cockatiel. The more time that is spent, and the more handling, the quicker the bird becomes confiding.

Rope Climbing

When you have succeeded in having your cockatiel climb a ladder, follow up by teaching it to climb a rope or walk a tightrope. Begin with rope (or chain) thick enough for the bird's grasp. Find a way to make the rope vertical and taut; then place the bird at the bottom and patiently push it up. Once the cockatiel understands what is expected of it, it will climb the rope each time it is put near it. If you do the same with the rope fixed in a horizontal position, the bird will walk your tightrope. Actually, it's probably better to accustom the bird to the horizontal rope first. Be patient; your bird may not pick up these tricks as fast as you'd like, so be sure it is not your fault it is not doing well.

Riding in a Car

One of the easiest tricks is to teach your cockatiel to ride on a small toy car equipped with a perch as you pull the car around. Let the bird become familiar with the toy for a few days. If necessary, show it how to hop onto the perch. With constant repetition, the bird will soon hop onto the perch (or into a toy without a perch) when brought to it.

Pulling a Toy

When you want your bird to pull a toy, just show it what you want it to do. The bird will soon learn that something is expected when a toy or other object is placed in its beak. Since cockatiels are attracted to shiny things, a metal bead-chain attached to the toy works nicely. All you need to do is provide guidance and repeat the action over and over again. Don't forget to supply a reward for success!

Once the three basic tricks have been mastered, what your bird can learn is limited only by your imagination and patience. There is no end to the surprises a young cockatiel will provide for you.

TALKING

As you begin to think about teaching your cockatiel to

TAMING AND TRAINING

talk, keep in mind that some birds are more adept at talking than others. There is a great deal of difference in the learning ability of each individual bird. This is one of the reasons for stressing the importance of getting to know your bird and its moods and working with the bird when it is most teachable. Regardless of the individuality of your bird, you can be assured that with perseverance just about any cockatiel, even an older one, can be taught to mimic at least a few words.

The actions taken in preparation for training are very important. No bird will be ready to talk unless it feels comfortable and relaxed in the company of its trainer. As you prepare to teach the first few words to your cockatiel, you must protect your bird from becoming frightened by other pets or noisy youngsters; you must especially guard the bird against sudden sounds and abrupt movements.

This is one reason why the location of the cage is so important. The bird should be placed where it is able to see what is going on, but the location must be safe enough and far enough away from the hustle and bustle of the household so that it will not become alarmed or distracted. Perhaps the most important ingredient of the training recipe is you. Give your bird attention and kindness so that it will come to love and trust you—and success is almost guaranteed. The sound of your voice and the attachment your pet is starting to develop for you are quite important.

The sex of the bird has no definite bearing on its ability to imitate. Cockatiels of both sexes have learned to talk. But you can expect that the younger the bird is, the more rapid will be its progress. The secrets of teaching a cockatiel to talk are patience, perseverance, and constant repetition. Aside from a few qualifiers, that's all there is to it.

Pulling a toy is a cute little trick that cockatiels are quick to learn. Always remember to reward your bird for success!

One must always remember that a talking bird does not reason and does not understand the words it repeats. The bird only mimics the words it hears and repeats only by rote. If you choose to teach your bird words that are

Fruits and vegetables are an essential part of your cockatiel's diet. Always feed these in moderation and be sure to have plenty of his regular diet available as well.

inappropriate for general use, you will have no one but yourself to blame when it embarrasses you. Talking birds seem to pick up swearing quite easily. This is because such expressions are usually spoken clearly and distinctly, often somewhat louder than the normal speech level.

When you begin to teach it to talk, chances for success will be enhanced if you use a louder voice than usual—remember that all birds belonging to the parrot family like noise and pay more attention to a loud voice than to a soft one. Up to this point you have attempted to gain your pet's confidence by using softly spoken words; now the only words spoken should be the ones you are trying to have the cockatiel learn. It's all right to continue to speak softly to the bird, but speak loudly, clearly, and distinctly during training sessions.

If you like talking to your bird and watching it learn new words, you can use modern training tools to effectively expedite the process. Have fun conversing with your feathered friend. Photo courtesy of Wordy Birds Products.

Some who have had a great deal of experience with cockatiels believe that talking lessons should be given while the bird is perched on the trainer's finger. Other experts feel that the practice distracts the attention of the bird and that teaching should be accomplished with the bird in the familiar and secure surroundings of its cage. You will have to decide which environment is the least distracting to your bird. There are trainers who feel the best way to gain the bird's attention is to conduct the training with the cage covered. This practice is not generally followed, although employing this method for the very first session of the day, as well as the last, is not without merit.

To actually teach the cockatiel to talk, the trainer should pick out just *one* word to start with. Begin with something simple, perhaps the bird's name or a single-syllable word, and repeat it several times. Say the word over and over again for a short period of time, then end the lesson. Do not insert other words or phrases into the conversation; doing so will only serve to confuse your pet. Repeat the word each time you pass the bird's cage.

Each time you repeat the word, use the same intonation; try not to change the way you repeat it. The first word you teach should be repeated slowly, with a pause between each repetition. Words that are strongly accented are preferred, at least in the beginning, as are higher pitched sounds.

Many cockatiels are inclined to whistle. This attempt at communication should not be encouraged, as many cockatiel owners have found that, however much they enjoyed the sound at first, with time it can be particularly annoying. Besides, the bird may be whistling instead of talking. Another cockatiel sound that may be mentioned is hissing. This is a normal response when a cockatiel is disturbed or frightened. As your cockatiel becomes accustomed to you, the hissing should disappear.

You will hear that some cockatiels have said their first word in a few weeks; don't be dismayed if it takes much longer for your bird to repeat its first word. Once it has mastered its first word, though, it will learn others more rapidly. Constant repetition is the basis of successfully teaching a cockatiel to speak. If you are teaching a phrase, when the next word is added, *always* repeat the preceding word or words before the new one. If you continue in this way, your cockatiel will soon amaze you with the extent of its vocabulary. You will also find that your bird will pick up and repeat words that have not been deliberately taught to it; these words or phrases will be those frequently repeated in its presence.

BREEDING COCKATIELS

Generally speaking, cockatiels are easy to breed. Once satisfied with a mate and nesting accommodations, eggs and young quickly follow. The other wonderful aspect of cockatiel breeding is that it takes place year round under the proper conditions. Most parrot and parrot-like birds are seasonal breeders and only produce young once or twice a year at the warmest times. The cockatiel, however, breeds all year and can produce a number of clutches before needing a rest.

Cockatiels are most prolific and have the highest number of fertile eggs in the spring and summer. The fall and winter months do not give the birds enough natural daylight needed to properly feed their chicks. The cold temperature of the wintertime also causes eggs to chill when birds come off the nest to feed and therefore the egg dies. Due to modern technology, artificial light and heat that simulates natural can be supplied to the birds so that these misfortunes do not take place.

To keep your birds healthy it is best to only breed them seasonally, however, the nest boxes must be completely removed from the cockatiels' view otherwise the birds will continue breeding. Try to only allow your cockatiel to raise two or three clutches of chicks per year to keep them healthy and full of vigor. Keep in mind that it is best to start off with only healthy stock. Obtain your pair of birds from a

Although some mutations are the result of inbreeding, closely related stock should not be bred together. Only very experienced breeders who have special knowledge of inbreeding and have a definite objective in view should breed their birds.

reputable pet shop and be certain that you obtain a guarantee of health with your birds. It would be a very wise decision to bring your new pair to the veterinarian's office within 48 hours of purchasing it so that the good health of the birds may be verified.

SELECTING THE PAIR

It is easy to distinguish the male and female apart in many cockatiel varieties through their appearance. Others can only be told apart by their actions, and even this is not always reliable. The normal (wild grey), lutino, pearl, grey whiteface, cinnamon whiteface, cinnamon, and silver varieties can all be sexed visually. In all of these varieties, except the lutino, the male has a prominent yellow or white coloration to his face while the female does not. The lutino cannot be sexed this way and one must rely on the wing patterning that can also be found on the other varieties mentioned. Upon opening the wing of your cockatiel, the inner portion will exhibit yellow barring if it is a female and no barring will be present if it is a male.

In addition to this, it must be mentioned that all birds must be old enough before it will be evident of what its sex is. All birds hatch and obtain the same duller coloration that the female displays. It is not until the bird's first molt that

BREEDING COCKATIELS

When two or more cockatiels are housed together, they will rarely breed.

has passed away, this is usually the only time they do so. It is not advisable to separate and re-pair your birds once mating has taken place because new mates are usually not accepted. Two cockatiels that have not been paired before do not always readily pair together. It is a wise idea to have several birds of opposite sexes together in the same cage and allow them to pair themselves up.

It is often better to pair a cockatiel that is an experienced breeder with one that has not bred before. If the young bird becomes slack in his or her responsibilities, the older one will often take over and set the example.

the adult coloration is evident and when sexing is possible.

The pearl cockatiel variety may be sexed in the same manner of the other varieties, however, after molting, the male of this variety loses his pearl and assumes a normal or cinnamon, or whatever color variety he may be, coloration. The female retains her pearl, so it is easy to visually tell what sex she is.

The pied varieties are difficult to sex. They are not distinguishable by their color or patterning. Careful observation of behavior and actions are usually the only way to be sure of what you are getting.

Since cockatiels are very affectionate birds, they form strong pair-bonds with their mates. Although they will accept another mate if theirs

BREEDING COCKATIELS

> Prior to the actual breeding season, prospective pairings should be made on paper with each bird's pedigree checked against the stock register.

BREEDING COCKATIELS

The placement of the nest is important. It should be easily accessible and convenient for the pair to come and go. It should also be located somewhere that the birds will feel secure.

It is often interesting to watch these birds court and pair and almost fall in love with one another. The male cockatiel will whistle and bob his head up and down quite comically to his female of choice—she will run away many times before finally giving her affections back to her mate in the form of preening and scratching. It is not long after this courtship that mating can be expected.

Be certain that the birds you choose are of good health, are fairly young and are of good feather. Sickly, old and plucked birds will not be able to produce healthy young.

THE NEST BOX

After you have selected your pair of cockatiels and they appear to get along well with each other, the next step is to acquire a nest box. A normal cockatiel nest box must be large enough to house a pair of cockatiels and its chicks—anywhere from three to eight birds. The proper sized nest box can be purchased from your local pet supply store. It will have an entrance hole located in the front of it with a smaller hole for a dowel below. The dowel should rest half-in and half-out of the nest in order to aid the cockatiels in and out of the nest.

Most cockatiel nest boxes are either rectangular or square and average 12-18in. square. For best results, hang the nest box from the outside of the cage and high up in a corner. A few of the cage bars may need to be removed in order to hang the box from the outside, however, this allows the birds the maximum amount of space within the cage.

There are several different opinions as to weather cockatiels require nesting material, however, most breeders recommend some pine shavings within the nest. It is debatable as to how much of this substance is needed, but a good cushion that can be easily pushed about by the pair will do. A small amount of water should be poured over the shavings so that the nest is not too dry. The water will provide the proper amount of humidity for the eggs to develop without drying out.

You can expect a pair of birds that is ready to breed to move into the nest box within one or two weeks of placing it in the cage. If your birds show no interest after this amount of time, they are either not ready for breeding or do not like the location of the nest. You can try to move the box to the other side of the cage or towards the back. Several tries to find the preferred location may be necessary.

Except when breeding is restricted to warmer months of the year, it is advised that nest boxes be made with tight joints and thick walls and bottom so that they can retain the maximum of heat.

BREEDING COCKATIELS

MATING

Breeding cockatiels should be at least one year of age. Younger birds are able to breed, but they do not seem competent in caring for their young.

The male cockatiel inspects the nest first and then invites the female in. After the female enters the box, she will begin to burrow into the nesting material and create a hollowed portion in which she will lay her eggs. The male will "court" his hen. He will sing, whistle, to her and feed her while she sits in the nest. There will be a lot of mutual preening, cooing, and cuddling during this time. It is amazing to see that birds can show genuine affection towards one another. Mating will soon take place.

When the hen is ready to mate, she will lower her back inviting the male to mount her. When he does this he will stand on her back and swing his tail from side to side until their vents meet. You can expect the first egg within a week of this mating. Cockatiels will breed in this matter several times a day until a full clutch of eggs—usually five—is laid.

EGG LAYING

It is amazing to see how quickly a female cockatiel lays her eggs after a nest box is provided and mating has taken place. Before she begins to lay her eggs, however, she will sleep outside the nest. It is not until she has laid her first egg that she continuously stays inside the box.

The usual size of the clutch is three to six eggs with an interval of one day between each egg. The male will spend some time inside the box with the hen, but will exit often to eat and return to feed his mate. Many male cockatiels share in the incubation duties, but the female incubates the majority of the eggs.

Nest boxes may be mounted in a number of ways. It is best to locate it high up in a corner, however, it may need to be moved so that your cockatiels accept it.

A week after the eggs are laid you can check their fertility by holding them up to a strong light. A fertile egg will appear half full and will have red veins beginning to run through it. If the egg is clear, you can assume it is infertile, but it would be best to wait a few more days and check the fertility again before discarding the eggs. There are many causes for infertile eggs, including improper diet, and this should be modified if you find an entire clutch is no good.

INCUBATION AND REARING OF THE CHICKS

Cockatiel eggs have an incubation period of 19-21 days. In cold weather the incubation process is at the longer end of time. The time it takes for a chick to break out of its shell can vary from 12-48 hours. If you feel that a

Cockatiel chicks appear to grow while you watch them. Within a few days they will double and triple in size.

Young birds need to exercise. To avoid overcrowding, remove individual youngsters away from their parents when they become ready. This is an excellent time for finger taming and training.

chick is having trouble breaking out of the shell, do not try to aid the bird. There is a vital membrane that cannot be torn and you may only harm the bird in your good efforts. The pair and the chick itself are usually more than capable of hatching with no outside assistance.

A newly hatched chick is very helpless and it cannot move around well nor lift its head. Its beak is also soft and pliable. The chick's eyes will be sealed and do not open until around the 12th day of life. Cockatiel chicks are covered in yellow fuzz—white fuzz if it is of the whiteface variety or an albino.

You will be aware that the first chick has hatched because you will hear faint chirping noises coming from within the nest box as the parents feed the chick. You should supply them with plenty of soft food at this time as they will need the extra food to feed the chicks. Soft food is extremely beneficial as it is easy for the birds to digest and regurgitate back up to feed back to the chicks. It is also very easy for the chicks to digest.

Newly hatched chicks cannot maintain their body temperature and therefore need a constant source of warmth—most likely their parents. These tiny chicks cannot withstand being left without warmth. Should a clutch of chicks be left by the parents to get chilled, it is best to remove them and place them in a brooder where they can be hand reared. It is not until the feathers begin to appear that the chick's are able to maintain their body temperature. Very often at this stage a number of chicks will huddle together for body warmth.

The chicks are fed hourly during the day, but most often they are left unfed during the night. This is because in the wild, cockatiels do not forage about during the night to search for food and likewise, they will not do so in captivity either. At first daylight, however, they will come off the nest to eat and quickly feed their chicks.

After about eight days of life the tiny eye slits of the chicks begin to open. Their pleasing little cheeps also turn harsher and angry. They begin to hiss and rock back and forth when a stranger approaches them.

It is a good idea to begin handling the chicks at this age as they are very impressionable. The parents will not mind, as long as you do not chase them off the nest to do so. There are plenty of times when the parents will be off their nest allowing you to sneak in the box and pick up a chick or two.

Around this age the cockatiel chick is ready to have an identification band placed on its leg. These bands are usually needed if the bird

A cockatiel chick requires constant brooding at this age because it cannot maintain its body temperature.

BREEDING COCKATIELS

is going to be shown later or to document the bird's lineage. If you are only doing this as a hobby, there is no need to band your youngsters.

The identification bands can be purchased from specialty shops and from bird clubs. Be certain to specify that the cockatiel sized bands are needed as bands come in an array of sizes and one that is too small will prove detrimental to your bird.

Cockatiel chicks will stay in the nest until they are approximately five weeks old. It is at this time that one or two may become inquisitive enough to fall out of the box. You can simply pick them up and place them back, but this will only work for a day or two. After that the young birds will be pros at getting out of the box and would rather be in the confines of the cage than in the crowded box.

Plenty of soft food should continue to be fed as the young birds will experiment and try to eat on their own. It is only about another week that they do so as the parent birds quickly tire and the young birds become independent. Once you are certain the young cockatiels are eating enough soft food on their own to maintain their own body weight, they may be removed from their parents' care.

It is about this time that the female will begin to lay a second clutch of eggs. If some stubborn six-week-old chicks have not left the nest, it is best to kick them out, otherwise they will interfere with the incubation process of the new eggs.

The baby cockatiel does not gape wide for food. The person hand feeding a cockatiel chick has to work the food through a narrow opening which makes rearing the young take a little longer than if done by the parents.

YOUR COCKATIEL'S GOOD HEALTH

Cockatiels are quite affectionate birds, and as an owner of one of these it is quite likely that you will, or already have, become quite attached to your pet. It is for this reason that you should try to keep your pet in his best health. Any deviation from the animal's normal good health is reason enough to call your veterinarian. Birds have very little fat stores and can quickly deteriorate once an illness sets in.

When your cockatiel is in good health he will sit with his feathers tight to his body, will be active, will have bright eyes and no discharge coming from his nose or mouth. He will also sleep on his perch with one leg tucked up into his body. A sick cockatiel will sit with his feathers fluffed away from his body trying to keep in his body temperature, will sleep for the better part of the day, will have loose droppings, watery discharge coming from his nose, eyes or mouth and will not be active. A bird that displays any or all of these symptoms should be regarded as ill, and proper medical attention should be sought.

It is advisable to have a "hospital" cage available and ready in case your bird should fall ill. A hospital cage is simply a smaller cage that restricts movement to a minimum and can have a heat source easily supplied to it. An ideal cage for this purpose is one that is solid on three sides with only a wire front. In a cage of this type, nothing can frighten the ill bird from the back or sides, and it can obtain its needed rest without being disturbed. A cage with three solid sides also does not allow heat to escape as would an all-wire cage.

Heat is very important in the recovery of ill birds, and it alone often can greatly improve the health of an ailing victim. Trying to keep its body temperature in causes the bird to expend a large amount of energy that it does not have. When you notice your cockatiel sitting fluffy, immediately transfer it to a hospital cage and supply it with a heat source that can warm it up to 85-90°F. This way the bird does not have to try to keep itself warm.

As being ill takes a great deal of energy out of a bird, it is important that the bird not be further stressed. Try to keep your sick pet as quiet as possible, do not make it search for its food, and follow your veterinarian's instructions to the letter. An ill bird can quickly deteriorate and time is very valuable. Do not return your bird to its regular accommodations until you have gradually removed the heat source and the bird has not shown any signs of illness for at least ten days. If you move your bird too quickly, a relapse could occur.

Quarantining your bird

Your pet cockatiel is a very important part of your life and you owe it to him to keep him in the best possible health.

> The best way to keep your cockatiel in his best health is to provide him with a good diet, clean accommodations and plenty of companionship.

A sick bird will show specific signs to warn you that it is not feeling well. Sitting with its wings fluffed out to hold in its body temperature, loose droppings and an overall decline in activity are all signs of the onset of illness. Should any of these symptoms manifest themselves, it would be best to move your bird to a hospital cage.

away from other stock is also imperative when an illness transpires. A 14 to 21-day quarantine period never hurt anyone's stock. It is always better to practice safe hygiene instead of taking chances. Likewise, any new stock that you acquire should be quarantined for a period of time before you introduce it to your present stock to prevent any illnesses entering your bird room.

Be certain that the hospital cage you used to house your ill bird in is completely sterilized after the bird has recovered. Everything should be cleaned and sterilized including the feeders and perches. Do this as soon as you remove the ill bird and keep the cage ready for the next time it may be needed.

Although proper hygiene and good care are your best defenses against ailments and illnesses affecting your stock, there are still ways that diseases find to enter. Other bird-owning friends are prime candidates for carrying diseases on their clothes and shoes into your bird room or home. It is for this reason that you must be very careful about who visits your pet or pets. You, too, can transport disease on your clothes from pet shops that you may have visited or other birds that you handled. Always wash your hands and change your clothes if you have been somewhere with other birds. Even though they did not appear ill to you, the other birds may still be harboring a disease that could be transferred to your stock.

Unfortunately, even though we take all the necessary precautions, an illness can still somehow manifest itself in our stock. The most common ailments and their symptoms are discussed here. It is important to remember that many illnesses can manifest very rapidly and can also display the same symptoms as other illnesses. It is therefore imperative that you contact your veterinarian immediately upon suspicion of your pet falling ill so that he may digest it correctly.

COLD

The common cold usually displays itself like many other illnesses. Your cockatiel will sit with his feathers fluffed out, will be less active and will have watery droppings. In conjunction with these symptoms, your cockatiel will

Be very careful about who comes to your home to visit your pets. Other bird-owning friends can easily carry disease on their clothing without even knowing it.

YOUR COCKATIEL'S GOOD HEALTH

also have long periods of sneezing.

If you suspect your cockatiel has a cold, immediately give it warmth and contact your veterinarian. A general antibiotic to add to the drinking water may be all that is needed.

CONJUNCTIVITIS

If you find your cockatiel is squinting, or not keeping his eye or eyes as wide open as normal, this is reason to suspect conjunctivitis. Upon close examination of the eyes, you will notice that they are very watery. A veterinary prescribed eye ointment is necessary to correct this condition. To administer this, the bird must be held restrictivly in your hand or a towel and the ointment must be placed directly into the eye. Follow the veterinarian's orders as to how often this must be done.

CONSTIPATION/DIARRHEA

If there is a lack of droppings in your bird's cage, you can guess that your bird is constipated. Very often the afflicted bird will peck repeatedly at the vent region as well. Constipation is usually the direct result of diet. In the same respect it can usually be corrected by diet as well. Consult your veterinarian if you suspect this to be your bird's problem.

Diarrhea is a symptom that often accompanies a variety of illnesses. It can also be caused by an improper diet, or poor water conditions. Many a bird can be helped by not supplying city water for it to drink. Unfortunately, our water supplies are often treated with chemicals that immediately affect our birds. Spring or distilled water is best to give to your stock at all times that way the water supply cannot be blamed as the culprit of the diarrhea. Since diarrhea can be the beginning of a more serious problem, consult your veterinarian on first noticing this symptom.

Eye infections require obtaining a prescription ointment from your veterinarian. This usually begins with watering of the eyes followed by the surrounding feathers appearing wet and possibly missing from the area.

EGG-BINDING

The inability for a female bird to expel an egg is called egg-binding. If this is not dislodged, the bird will not be able to expel waste products and will develop a toxemia which ultimately leads to death. If you suspect your female to be egg-bound you must act fast if you are to save her life. Do not try to catch the bird for this may break the egg inside her—causing peritonitis and death. Leave her as calm as you can, supply a heat source. If the heat has not helped after one

YOUR COCKATIEL'S GOOD HEALTH

When a cockatiel falls ill, it is important to separate him from other stock because they may become offensive towards the weaker animal.

not have the muscle strength to pass a fully formed egg, and thus she will become egg-bound.

Egg-binding is a very serious condition that must be treated immediately if your cockatiel is to survive.

FEATHER PICKING

Feather picking is not always an illness, but more of a condition or a poor state of mind. There are many reasons for this condition, and only through trial and error can the true reason be found. Inadequate diet, lighting, temperature and humidity conditions and companionship are the top causes for this mutilating vice. A perfectly normal and happy bird suddenly begins to tear into its own feathers. He either shreds them up and leaves them on his body to look unsightly, or completely tears them out of his body and leaves bare patches of skin showing through. An inadequate diet is easy enough to fix to a better one, and inadequate lighting is also easy enough to fix, as well as temperature and humidity, however, boredom or lack of companionship is not so easy to correct.

Sometimes no matter how much attention or no matter how many toys your bird has, it still wants, and needs, more to thrive. Some birds just become demanding that way. It is unfortunate to see owners trying every remedy possible with none helping. Owners are usually left to face the fact that their bird will have to live the rest of its life denuded of its feathers and happy with the attention and toys it has.

hour's time, as gently as possible, catch her and lubricate her vent with olive oil. If the oil treatment does not work, your veterinarian may be able to gently work the egg out with his hands, however, it is probably too late to save the bird's life.

There are several things that can be done to prevent egg-binding. One is to supply plenty of calcium for your female. Calcium forms the hard outer shell of the egg, and if there is not enough in your bird's diet the shell will be too soft for the bird to pass it. The other thing that proves to be a common cause of egg-binding is lack of exercise. You must be certain that your female cockatiel is exercised plenty before she begins a breeding program. If the female is not in proper breeding condition she will

Broken wings must be set, preferably by a veterinarian, to heal properly. At times, a wing may remain slightly drooped if not set correctly or if sprained. During the healing time of this injury the bird should not be permitted to exercise much.

YOUR COCKATIEL'S GOOD HEALTH

Veterinarians have designed plastic collars for feather picking birds. These collars are so designed that the bird cannot reach its feathers, yet can eat normally and basically get around its cage normally as well. While these collars do not prove to end feather picking, they do stop the bird from doing further damage to itself.

Even after the cause for the feather picking has been found, it has often become a terrible habit that is difficult to correct. Bad-tasting sprays that are available from pet stores can sometimes remedy the situation.

If feather picking is a problem that affects your cockatiel, bring him to an avian vet who can help remedy the situation as soon as possible.

Lice and mites are commonly contracted during breeding times. Try to keep your birds' accommodations very clean during this time to avoid these pesky creatures.

Breeding birds should have their nails filed so that the eggs they lay are not accidentally broken.

LICE AND MITES

A bird that is suffering from these parasites will often scratch and itch. These external parasites often live in the tiny nooks and crevices of the cages and they emerge to feed on the bird. There are several types of mites and lice that can be found on your bird and they can all be easily eliminated with the proper treatment. Several treatments will need to be made to be certain that all eliminated.

OVERGROWN BEAK AND CLAWS

Overgrown beak and claws can prove to be hazardous to your cockatiel. If the beak grows too long, it can inhibit the bird's eating ability. Many owner's do not even realize this occurs until it is too late. Since there is a blood supply that runs through the beak, it is important that you do not attempt to trim this back yourself. Your veterinarian should be contacted and he can show you how to go about this so that you can perform the task at home.

Not all birds need to have their beak trimmed. Keep this in mind when you begin to worry that you have had your cockatiel for a while and haven't had his beak trimmed.

Most birds, however, do need to have their nails trimmed. Although they can gradually wear these down on their own cage on their perches, they probably do need to have their nails trimmed at least twice a year. Again, take your cockatiel to the veterinarian and have him show you how to safely perform this task.

SUGGESTED READING

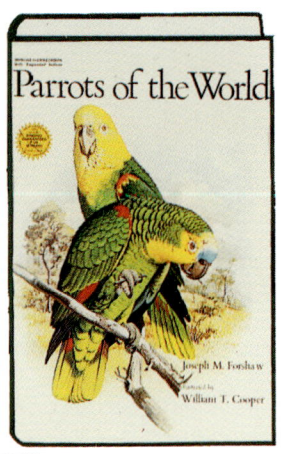

PS-753
PARROTS OF THE WORLD
by J.M. Forshaw
Almost 500 species and subspecies are presented here., 584 pages, over 300 full-color plates.

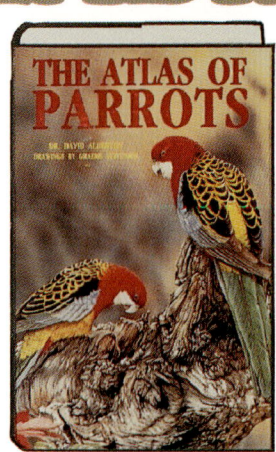

H-1109
ATLAS OF PARROTS
by David Alderton, Illustrations by G. Stevenson
Illustrated coverage of every species and subspecies of parrot in the world. 544 pages, over 300 full-color plates.

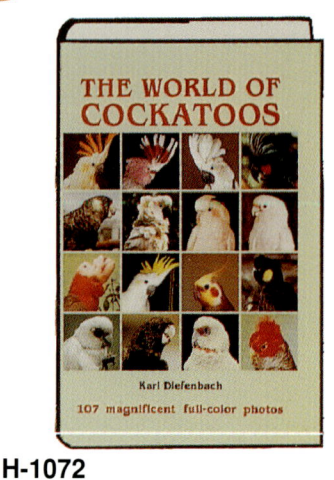

H-1072
THE WORLD OF COCKATOOS
by Karl Diefenbach
A highly informative book detailing everything the Cockatoo lover needs to know. 208 pages, 80 full color photos.

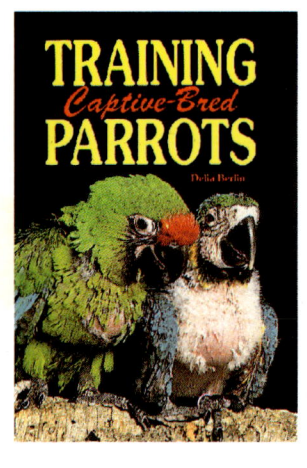

TS-242
TRAINING CAPTIVE-BRED PARROTS
by Delia Berlin
Most of the parrots sold today were bred in captivity and hand reared. They are much easier to handle, tame and train than wild-caught birds, and this book tells and shows parrot owners how to take advantage of that important feature. 128 pages, over 170 full-color photos.

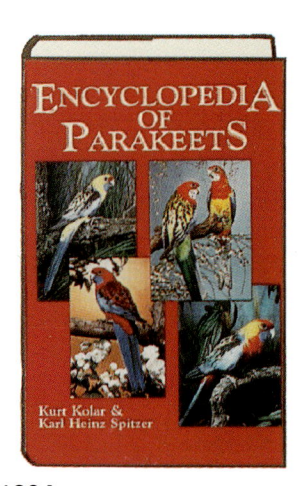

H-1094
ENCYCLOPEDIA OF PARAKEETS
by K. Kolar and K.H. Spitzer
This thorough coverage ranges from little known species to the familiar budgerigar and cockatiel. 223 pages with many full color photos.

KW-001
TAMING AND TRAINING COCKATIELS
by Risa Teitler
This exciting book is designed for maximum information value and dramatic eye appeal. Coverage includes training tips, special behavior problems and other valuable insights. 128 pages and over 92 full-color photos.